Germantown Academy
Lower School Library

Roots of the Republic

ROOTS OF THE REPUBLIC

Dr. Gary D. Hermalyn, Project Editor
Brother C. Edward Quinn, Consulting Editor
Professor Lloyd Ultan, Consulting Editor

Signers of the Declaration of Independence
by Brother C. Edward Quinn

Signers of the Constitution of the United States
by Brother C. Edward Quinn

The First Senate of the United States 1789-1795
by Richard Streb

The First House of Representatives and the Bill of Rights
by George Lankevich

Chief Justices of the United States
by Geroge Lankevich

Presidents of the United States
by Lloyd Ultan

Roots of the Republic

The First Senate of the United States 1789-1795

VOLUME 3

Richard Streb

GROLIER EDUCATIONAL
Sherman Turnpike, Danbury, Connecticut

Published 1996 by Grolier Educational, Danbury, Connecticut
© 1996 by The Bronx County Historical Society

Set ISBN 0-7172-7608-2
Volume ISBN: 0-7172-7612-0
Library of Congress number 95-082224

All rights reserved. No part of this book may be used or reproduced in any manner whatsoever or transmitted in any form or by any means, electronic or mechanical, including photocopying, recording, or any information storage and retrieval system, without written permission from the copyright owner except in the case of brief quotations embodied in critical articles and reviews.

For information, address the publisher:
Grolier Educational, Danbury, Connecticut 06816.

Cover design by Smart Graphics
Book design by Henry C. Meyer Jr.

TABLE OF CONTENTS

Dedication vii
Acknowledgments ix
Introduction xi
The Creation of the Senate 1
Powers Granted to Congress 7
The Election for the First Senate 10
First Senate Meeting Dates and Other Data 12
Meeting Locations for the Senate 14
First Senate Issues 17
The First Senators

> *Connecticut*
> Oliver Ellsworth 26
> William Samuel Johnson 29
>
> *Delaware*
> Richard Bassett 34
> George Read 36
>
> *Georgia*
> William Few 40
> James Gunn 43
>
> *Maryland*
> Charles Carroll of Carrollton 46
> John Henry 48
>
> *Massachusetts*
> Tristram Dalton 52
> Caleb Strong 54
>
> *New Hampshire*
> John Langdon 58
> Paine Wingate 61
>
> *New Jersey*
> William Paterson 66
> Philemon Dickinson 69
> Jonathan Elmer 71

New York
    Rufus King 74
    Philip Schuyler 78

North Carolina
    Benjamin Hawkins 82
    Samuel Johnston 85

Pennsylvania
    William Maclay 90
    Robert Morris 93

Rhode Island
    Theodore Foster 98
    Joseph Stanton 101

South Carolina
    Pierce Butler 104
    Ralph Izard 107

Virginia
    William Grayson 112
    John Walker 114
    James Monroe 116
    Richard Henry Lee 119

THE FIRST SENATE IN PROFILE 123

PROFILE REFERENCE CHART 126

NOTES ON THE BILL OF RIGHTS 127

THE SENATORS IN ORDER OF STATE
    CONSTITUTIONAL RATIFICATION 130

CHRONOLOGY 132

NOTES 135

BIBLIOGRAPHY 136

PORTRAIT CREDITS 138

ABOUT THE AUTHOR 139

INDEX 141

DEDICATION

To some of the great teachers I have known:

Sister Anita, SSJ., Salo Wittmayer Baron, Ruth Benedict, Patricia Driscoll, James Eder, George Fouron, Thomas O'Donnell, Nathaniel Peffer, Nina Pozgar, Mannie Raff, Sandy Redock, Sandy Scarpinito, Linda Skidmore, my sister, Sister Pius, SSJ., my brother, Robert Streb, my wife, Rosemary Laurer Streb, Jack Trout, Gene Weltfish, Peter White, Sister Joan Uhlen, M.M...

...and to two caring and knowledgeable administrators:

Bernard Schneider and Christopher Vagts.

...and to a computer teacher who said, "Of Course You Can," Marcia Bannerjee.

...and to my most competent and hardworking editors, Prof. Lloyd Ultan, Dr. Gary Hermalyn, Mr. Dan Eisenstein.

...and finally to a public servant of the New York State Department of Education, knowledgeable, dedicated, untiring in her efforts to improve education, Loretta Carney.

ACKNOWLEDGMENTS

I must extend a hearty thank you to the people who assisted me in research for this project at: The Bronx County Historical Society, The Bronx, New York, the Columbia University Library, New York, New York; Milbank Memorial Library, Teachers College, Columbia University, New York, New York; Rundel Library, Rochester, New York; the University of Rochester Library, Rochester, New York; the National Portrait Gallery, Washington, D.C. and The Rhode Island Historical Society, Providence, Rhode Island.

INTRODUCTION

In 1957, Senator John F. Kennedy chaired a Senate committee which selected the five most outstanding senators in American history to serve as models for what "the good and effective senator should be." At the time, no one called this study an attempt to build a Senate Hall of Fame, but, for many, that seemed to be a good way to categorize the results. They chose Henry Clay of Kentucky (1777-1852), Daniel Webster of Massachusetts (1782-1852), John Caldwell Calhoun of South Carolina (1782-1850), Robert LaFollette Sr. of Wisconsin (1855-1925), and Robert A. Taft Sr. of Ohio (1889-1953).

Clay, Webster, and Calhoun served in the first half of the nineteenth century, a time when the Senate became the most powerful body in the government. In those years, the decisions made, largely through compromise, resolved, for a time, many major differences. These included: the nature and extent of the Constitution, the relations between state and federal governments, slavery, tariffs, economic development, and foreign policy. All of these issues had serious implications for the country's future.

LaFollette Sr. and Taft Sr. were from the first half of the twentieth century, one hundred years later. Their public life spanned the years 1906 to 1953. While the Senate was no longer preeminent, it played a much more important part in national life than does the Senate in the closing years of the twentieth century, yet the same paramount issues will have a familiar ring today. During their era, the Senate faced many major problems: fighting wars, maintaining peace, and surviving a depression. Much time was also spent in the search for social, racial, and economic justice, and in building programs to save the environment. Issues, such as the tariff, were resolved when the government, under the New Deal, moved toward free trade and developed reciprocal trade agreements. The Senate had some problems of its own that demanded resolution.

However, though none of the first senators were selected by the committee, that does not in any way diminish their accomplishments. It was that first Senate, assembled in New York City in the old City Hall, which shaped the Senate and built a government. At the time, neither the city of Washington, nor the Senate chamber of the national Capitol, existed. The meeting room and the city where the first senators played their historic roles were far removed and far different from those in which the five chosen men held sway, yet the challenges faced by the first Senate were no less difficult. To some, they might have even seemed insurmountable.

England had not completely accepted the fact that the United States intended to maintain its independence. Therefore, they were violating provisions of the peace treaty which had ended the Revolutionary War.

There were 100,000 American settlers west of the Appalachians by 1790, and their survival and loyalty to the new government depended on its ability to secure access to the port of New Orleans. However, the Spanish did not respect the new nation's borders nor its sovereignty. Furthermore, they owned the city of New Orleans, and the port at the mouth of the Mississippi River, where they could, and did, cut off all shipments.

The Indians, defending their land, were seen as a menace to the frontier. Population growth and constant expansion by the United States led to frequent conflict and made life dangerous. It was apparent that the new nation needed an adequate defense establishment.

To add to the difficulties, the country's finances were in poor shape. First of all, it was owed about $22 million by the various states, second, it owed over $42 million to other nations, and finally it owed $54 million to many of its citizens. The prospects of repaying the debt were not readily apparent. The government had to find ways to pay the debt, gain recognition from foreign governments, and establish regular trade relationships with all nations. It was clear that in order to raise money to support the government and establish the international credit of the United States, a financial structure had to be devised.

To have truly united states, the complex relationships between branches of the federal government and between the federal and state governments had to be agreed upon. The limits of federal and state power had to be defined. Protocol for contact with the president and the new government officials needed to be developed. Most important was the fact that the people had been promised that a bill of rights would be added to the Constitution once it had been ratified.

All the senators, with widely varying backgrounds, beliefs, personalities and agendas, had to work together to achieve the common goal of solving those problems, while inventing their government. Everything the country had to do was for the first time, since there were no precedents. In all these monumental tasks, each branch of the new government had a role to play. The role of the senators in the first Senate is the subject of this book.

The Creation of the Senate

Though the structure and goals of the country were novel, the Senate of the United States was not an original creation. There were many historical models available to the members of the Constitutional Convention. For example, the Delian League, established by the city-states of ancient Greece, was organized to deal with problems common to its members. The League was charged with providing for the common defense. The rules for operation were drawn by the member states and were quite democratic. Each member city-state sent a delegate to represent its interests and to vote accordingly.

Benjamin Franklin's proposal for colonial unity, the Albany Plan of Union, in 1754, was modeled on the structure and process of the Iroquois Confederacy. Some historians suggest that the idea of a federal union can be traced directly to the principles found in the Iroquois Confederacy's "Great Law of Peace," since one of the principles used to structure the Senate paralleled those of the Iroquois.

Before the United States of America had its government as we know it today there had been three attempts at seeking a common ground for the "united" colonies, as well. These included the First Continental Congress, which was composed of representatives, from most of the colonies, who deliberated for seven weeks from September 5, to October 26, 1774. It was not a legislative body but one designed to share views in the hope of finding sufficient agreement for unified action.

The Second Continental Congress met in May of 1775. All thirteen colonies were represented. The most important action they took was to select George Washington to head the military forces that had been assembled to defend a besieged Boston. They also created a plan for a new government, the Articles of Confederation, which was not adopted until 1781. The Articles of Confederation provided for a league of friendship. Thirteen independent states were joined for common action in dealing with their problems. That Confederation Congress had no president, no power of taxation and no national court. This feeble government could advise and make requests of the independent states but could not command or enforce any decision. Though it somehow managed to "run" the fledgling country for eight years, from 1781 to 1789, it was clearly inadequate to provide security for the states and to protect the property of the landowners. These shortcomings provided the impetus to create a central federal government. That government was given the power to tax, some authority over the states, a President as executive head of the law enforcing branch, a bicameral or two-house law making body and authority to create a national court system to interpret the laws. The ideas shaping the Senate have also come, in part, from the writings of Locke and Montesquieu, as well as those of many other political writers. Essentially, the United States Senate combines features of two important models. The Senate of ancient Rome provided the intellectual rationale for the role and substance of the United States Senate. The House of Lords, in England's Parliament, provided much of the form and operational structure.

These were no small matters. Exactly how the national legislature should be elected and structured took the Constitutional Convention half the summer of 1787. Finally, it was agreed to write into the constitution that, "All legislative powers herein granted shall be vested in a Congress of the United States, which shall consist of a Senate and a House of Representatives." A month after it was approved it was discussed and voted upon a second time, whereupon it was approved again, unchanged. However, while the wording was approved, its actual implementation presented a fundamental problem. Since the "legislative" power is literally the "law making" power, they could pass laws that might put limits on the states and state laws. Since it was the "united" states, that were the basis of the new nation, state interests were always paramount in the debates at the Constitutional Convention. Questions about political power and governmental authority were discussed in terms of the impact upon the states. The Senate was expected to be the voice for, and protector of, those interests. Giving up states' rights caused some anguish, especially for the smaller states with fewer representatives. Therefore, while authority over state laws had been approved, it was later disapproved. Midway through the convention, the "Great Compromise" was effected. To properly protect state's interests, the Senate was to have equal representation from all states. Each would elect two senators, providing two votes to a state. With this change, and after much discussion, it was approved again.

Thus, the wording in the Constitution gave us our "Congress," which comes from the Latin word *congressus* - "meeting." The meeting consists of the members of each of the two "houses" during a session. The term "house" itself is a holdover from the British system. They referred to their "House of Lords" as "the upper house," because it had fewer members and more restrictive qualifications for membership than the "House of Commons," which was thus called the "lower house." We have adopted that practice as well. Our Senate was given the unofficial English-style name, "upper house," since it is restricted to only two senators per state, no matter what its size or population might be, and there are other restrictions on senators, as well. Our "lower house," which was deliberately given the name "House of Representatives," is based on the population of each state, as determined by an official census, or headcount.

"Congress" always refers to both houses combined. However, since both function independently, often even in opposition, it is necessary to say Senate when referring to an action of that body to distinguish it from something involving only the House of Representatives.

Protection from the new central government was one thing, but protection from the public at large was another matter entirely. Soon after the problem of how to share the power between the states and the central government was resolved, other issues surfaced. There was concern about mobs or common people taking charge of the legislature and passing laws that would take property from those better off and spreading it around to the masses. This presented quite a challenge for a developing democracy.

One conception of the Senate, showing the Roman influence, was that it would consist of older, more successful individuals who would take a more conservative view of property ownership. It was further assumed that state legislators electing the senators would more likely be the wealthy and powerful people within each state or, at least, they would be men with similar class interests. By the age of thirty, it was assumed that a man would have achieved some financial success and therefore would have a stake in preserving the status quo. The following additional restrictions were placed on membership for the exclusive "upper house." It was resolved that the senators were to be chosen by state legislators, had to be thirty years of age, an inhabitant of the state at the time of the election and nine years a citizen. This last point would be an issue that stood in the way of one man's nearly successful bid to become a senator. The times, the places and the manner of holding elections for senators and representatives were to be prescribed by the state legislatures.

Once the Senate was functioning it would face the problem of how to prevent the loss of all experience and wisdom from the seasoned members in any given election. The model that seemed most logical would have one-third of the senators being elected by the state legislators (not directly by the people, as we do today) every two years. Thus, two-thirds of the senators would always be in office, while one third were presenting themselves to the state legislators for election. This system seemed to guarantee stability, while offering the best balance of both continuity and gradual change.

However, since this was the first Senate, the members were all to be elected at the same time. Some way to divide it into thirds had to be devised. To start the sequence, members were to be arranged into three classes. The terms of those in Class 1 would expire at the end of the first Congress in March 1791. The terms of those in Class 2 would be four years, or until the end of the second Congress in March 1793. The last and luckiest would serve the full six years, or until the end of the third Congress, in 1795.

The twenty senators present on May 15, 1789, drew lots from a cleverly arranged lottery that assured that no class would contain more than one member per state and that there would be geographical spread as well. When the other senators arrived they were required to choose lots in a way that would retain the desired balance.[1] Thus, with two-thirds always holding a seat, the Senate is a continuous body, with gradual change.

Of course, that strength, being a continuing body, is unfortunately a weakness, as well. It is difficult to change the rules governing procedures of a continuous group while it is in continuous operation. It is hard to overhaul an engine while it is running.

The "upper house" was a well-oiled machine. As an exclusive "club," beholden to the legislators and untouchable by the common man, it had built-in arrogance and ample opportunities for corruption. It was not until the Senate reached a low in public esteem and in venality in the early years of the twentieth century that a public outcry resulted in a reform of its method of election. The senators were too remote from the populace and not accountable enough. Direct election of senators by the people's vote came with the seventeenth amendment, in 1913.

The "lower house," on the other hand, was more accountable. Since members of the House of Representatives served for two years all of them stood for election at the same time and were elected by popular vote. Since the entire House of Representatives comes up for election every two years, when it assembles it is considered a new body. Consequently, the rules there can be reconsidered each time and are somewhat easier to change. Wisdom and experience are not lost, because many members are reelected. Hopefully they are the best of the lot.

Since all congressional terms are for two years, Americans elect a new Congress in November of even-numbered years, each of the two denoted as a first and a second session. The first Congress was an exception since it had to wait for some laggard states to ratify the Constitution. Thus, it met in three sessions.

The Congress was directed to assemble at least once a year, originally on the first Monday in December. As technology and transport improved, and it was possible to determine election results more quickly, it became feasible to shorten the time between election and inauguration for all officials. The twentieth amendment, proposed by Senator George Norris of Nebraska, changed the date when Congress ended and began its annual meetings. Beginning on January 3, 1933, the old Congress ended and the new one took office.

The Constitution gives each house the power and responsibility to judge the qualifications of its members and the correctness of election results. Each house is also directed to make its own rules of procedure and to decide when to punish a member for disorderly behavior. There are four degrees of punishment for a recalcitrant senator: denouncement, reprimand, censure, and expulsion; if two-thirds of the members agree, they can expel a member.

The Senate, as well as the House, is required by the Constitution to keep a record of its proceedings and to publish it. To these ends, the *Congressional Record* became available in most public libraries and is now instantly accessible by anyone using a computer, through various online services. Similarly, the once secret proceedings inside the Senate chamber are now broadcast, by cable television, to the populace.

Both Houses are required to agree on a date for adjournment. The Constitution gives the president the power to convene both houses or either one of them on extraordinary occasions and if they cannot agree on a time to adjourn he may set the time to adjourn.

Senators, like Representatives, receive a legally fixed salary paid by the federal government. On August 26, 1789, the first Compensation Bill was passed after heated debate. It provided for a salary of six dollars per day for senators.

Both houses enjoy what is called "congressional immunity." The members are not subject to arrest while on the way to, or from, or while attending a session, except in cases of treason, felony, or breach of peace. Further, they are afforded an exceptionally generous implementation of the first amendment. They have unrestricted freedom of speech. They cannot be arrested for any speech or debate and are immune from any libel suit based on those speeches. There was one very important prohibition on both houses. No senator or representative may hold any other civil office for the United States during his term in Congress. This was designed to prevent any conflict of interest.

POWERS GRANTED TO CONGRESS

The vice-president of the United States is the presiding officer of the Senate, in which capacity he has a vote only when there is a tie. This is the only assignment given to the office of the vice-president by the Constitution. John Adams, the first vice-president, said that the office was the most useless ever devised by the mind of man.

The Senate was authorized to choose other officers and a president *pro tempore* to take the vice-president's place in his absence.

Only the House of Representatives can charge (impeach) a government official with misconduct. On the other hand, only the Senate can hear those charges (hold a trial) and find guilt or innocence.

The powers delegated to Congress are found in Article I Section 8 of the Constitution. As part of Congress, the Senate, along with the House of Representatives, has the following powers:

To lay and collect Taxes, Duties, Imposts and Excises, to pay the Debts and provide for the common Defense and general Welfare of the United States...;

To borrow Money on the credit of the United States;

To regulate Commerce with foreign Nations, and among the several States, and with the Indian Tribes;

To establish an uniform Rule of Naturalization, and uniform laws on the subject of Bankruptcies throughout the United States;

To coin Money, regulate the value thereof, and foreign Coin, and fix the Standard of Weights and Measures;

To provide for the Punishment of counterfeiting the securities and current Coin of the United States;

To establish Post Offices and post Roads;

To promote the Progress of Science and useful Arts, by securing for limited Times to Authors and inventors the exclusive Right to their respective Writings and Discoveries;

To constitute Tribunals inferior to the supreme Court;

To define and punish Piracies and Felonies committed on the high Seas, and Offenses against the Law of Nations;

To declare War, grant Letters of Marque and Reprisal, and make Rules concerning Captures on Land and Water;

To raise and support Armies, but no appropriation for that use shall be for a longer term than two years;

To provide and maintain a Navy;

To make Rules for the Government and Regulation of the land and naval Forces;

To provide for calling forth the Militia to execute the Laws of the Union, suppress Insurrections, and repel Invasions;

To provide for organizing, arming, and disciplining the Militia, and for governing such Part of them as may be employed in the Service of the United States, reserving to the States respectively, the Appointment of the Officers, and the Authority of training the Militia according to the discipline prescribed by Congress;

To exercise exclusive Legislation in all Cases whatsoever, over [the District of Columbia] and to exercise like Authority over all Places purchased by the Consent of the Legislature of the State in which the Same shall be, for the erection of Forts, Magazines, Arsenals, dock-Yards, and other needful Buildings; —And

To make all Laws which shall be necessary and proper for carrying into Execution the foregoing Powers, and all other Powers vested by this Constitution in the Government of the United States, or in any department or officer thereof.

It is necessary to draw attention to one of the Senate's most important functions which is found in Article II, Section 2, dealing with the powers and duties of the president. Here we find this statement:

The President "shall have Power, **by and with the advice and consent of the Senate**, to make Treaties, provided two-thirds of the Senators present concur; and he shall nominate, **and by and with the advice and consent of the Senate**, shall appoint Ambassadors, other public Ministers and Consuls, Judges of the supreme court, and all other Officers of the United States, whose Appointments are not herein otherwise provided for, and which shall be established by Law: but the Congress may by Law vest the Appointment of such inferior Officers, as they think proper, in the President alone, in the Courts of Law, or in the Heads of Departments." (Emphasis added)

This provision clearly shows the way in which the delegates to the Constitutional Convention viewed the Senate. The senators' good judgment and mature wisdom were to be employed in these crucial matters. In fact, they were to do more than approve or disapprove treaties and appointments. They were to be directly involved with the president's decisions, which were explicitly conveyed with the words "**by and with the Advice and Consent of the Senate.**" Undoubtedly, the Founding Fathers wanted them to have a say in the process of writing treaties and selecting powerful officials.

THE ELECTION FOR THE FIRST SENATE

Organizing The Election

On June 21, 1788, when New Hampshire became the ninth state to ratify, the Constitution of the United States of America became the law of the land. The Congress, under the Articles of Confederation, still the official government, set the first Wednesday in January 1789, as a date to select presidential electors. The electors were to cast ballots for the first president on the first Wednesday in February.

It also notified states to prepare elections for the new Senate and House of Representatives. It set March 4, 1789, as the date for the new Congress to assemble.

The Confederation Congress completed its work, packed its bags, and went home. This is one of few examples in history, of a government surrendering power peacefully, without coercion, then passing from the scene.

The Congressional Elections

The Senate elections were once conducted in the state legislatures where the American people had no direct voting rights. While the people did vote for their state legislators, who then voted for the senators, the elections for federal senators were held behind closed doors. This made the Senate one step removed from the people and the elections went almost unnoticed by the public at large. Most states held those senatorial elections earlier than the House of Representatives elections. That gave defeated candidates a chance to run for a House seat, if they so desired.

The House elections did not go unnoticed. The electioneering and voting, in 1789, was a public event which caused much excitement and popular involvement. Public debates were held, articles were written and speeches were made.

The essentially secret senatorial elections were often complex and full of political quicksand. Nowhere was this more evident than in the New York State Legislature. Its Senate was controlled by the Federalists, who were in favor of adopting the Constitution, but the Assembly was controlled by the Antifederalists, who wished to defeat adoption of the Constitution. The two bodies fought bitterly over whether to elect the senators in a joint session or by meeting separately. Each wanted to elect senators who supported their beliefs. The Assembly was larger and had more votes, thus, in joint voting, they could outvote the smaller Senate and get their people in. If they met separately, each house would have one vote. Mired in this quicksand, unable to agree, the Legislature adjourned and the state remained without representation in the first Senate during the crucial and formative four months of the first session. Only after state elections put both houses safely in Federalist control did the legislature meet together and elect senators, in July 1789.

Although their members were elected, neither house of Congress could begin organizing and operating until it had a quorum, according to the new Constitution. To protect the rights of all members, the Constitution defined a quorum as a majority. The House of Representatives had achieved its quorum on April 1, 1789. The Senate was not as prompt or successful.

Figuring the quorum should have been simple, since the Constitution had come into official existence when nine states ratified. With two Senators from each state, for a total of eighteen, only ten would have been required for a Senate quorum. However, Virginia and New York ratified the Constitution on June 26, 1788, **after** the order to hold elections was given by the old Confederation Congress. This made it eleven states that had ratified, raising the total to twenty-two senators, requiring twelve to make a simple majority. Since only eight answered the first call on March 4, by law, the Senate could not begin working until four more arrived to make a quorum.

Besides the New York legislature's postponed election, a severe snow storm in some states delayed some arrivals and others had personal reasons for not leaving home at that time. This meant that the House of Representatives was the only functioning part of the new government. The senators who were present, stressing the need to hurry, sent urgent messages to their fellow members. They trickled in until Richard Henry Lee, from Virginia, became the twelfth senator, giving them a quorum on April 6. The first Senate could begin its work. When the House of Representatives had achieved its quorum on April 1, some wags had noted it was April Fool's Day!

First Senate Meeting Dates and Other Data

Eight senators appeared on March 4, 1789. They met each day, but adjourned until a quorum could be reached. After more than a month, they finally had that quorum on April 6, 1789.

The first order of business was to elect officers and then to count the electoral votes for president and vice-president. This was done in a joint session meeting in the hall of the Senate chamber.

The officers of the first Senate were:

President of the Senate — Vice-President John Adams

John Adams assumed the chair of the Senate on April 21, 1789.

President *Pro Tempore* — Senator John Langdon, New Hampshire.

The members of the House of Representatives are elected for two-year terms; thus, Congress is numbered to conform to the two-year election. The First Congress was divided into three separate sessions due to the late ratification of the constitutions by some states.

The dates were as follows:

1st session — March 4, 1789 to September 29, 1789

2nd session — January 4, 1790 to August 12, 1790

3rd session — December 6, 1790 to March 3, 1791

Senators are elected for six-year terms and the constitution provided for one-third to be elected every two years. On May 15, 1789, the Senate, consisting of the first twenty senators who were present, drew lots to determine the classes into which the membership should be divided, with these results:

First Senate Meeting Dates and Other Data

Class 1 Term expired March 3, 1791	Class 2 Term expired March 3, 1793	Class 3 Term expired March 3, 1795
Carroll	Bassett	Gunn
Dalton	Butler	Henry
Ellsworth	Few	Johnson
Elmer	Lee	Izard
Maclay	Strong	Langdon
Read	Paterson	Morris
Grayson	Wingate	

VICE-PRESIDENT JOHN ADAMS
President of the First Senate

Meeting Locations for the First Senate

Many serious issues would divide the Senate in these early days. None was more contentious and took longer to resolve than the question of where the permanent seat of government should be located. Many months were spent on this issue and it was particularly emotional and heavy with implications for the future development of the nation. There were two main camps.

One of these comprised the agricultural interests and those who thought, like Jefferson, that the strength of the nation depended upon independent, land-owning farmers. The wanted a central location, preferring a site on the Potomac River, near the approximate center of the country at that time.

On the other side stood Hamilton and the commercial and shipping interests who wanted the capital located in New York City, the financial and industrial center of the nation. They believed that New York was the location that would foster capitalist activity and industrial growth. The differences between these factions was a recurrent theme throughout the early years of the first Senate.

Complicating matters further were others who held out for a site that would assure them of personal profit. Robert Morris, a senator from Pennsylvania, is an example of one who let his personal interests dictate his choice of location. He swapped several farms in western Pennsylvania for land around the Falls of the Delaware River which had some scattered support as the capitol. He did a lot of dealing behind the scenes to gain support for this position. In addition there were a small number of men who held out for a capital which, if located in their local area, would bring some benefit to the region. There were deep-rooted, sectional jealousies evident in the debate. Finally, as a way out of the dilemma, New York was picked as a temporary capital.

The long struggle to decide the permanent location of the new capital had a few good side effects. One of these occurred in New York City, where some well-heeled businessmen spent considerable amounts of money to restore the old City Hall to its original elegance. The Common Council of the city chose architect Pierre L'Enfant, the man who would later design the city of Washington, D.C., to make the changes. The work was not yet completed when the opening day for the new Congress arrived.

With its new-found status, the building at the corner of Wall and Nassau Streets became known as Federal Hall. The Senate chamber was on the second floor. It was a carpeted room forty feet long by thirty feet wide. The high arched ceiling was brightly painted with thirteen stars surrounding a shining sun. On the walls hung portraits of Louis XVI and Marie Antoinette. They had been gifts from the French government to New York City at a time when relationships between France and United States were more harmonious. There were tall windows, a fireplace with mantels of polished marble and an elevated dais for the presiding officer's chair that sat under a canopy of crimson cloth. This was a room worthy of the high purpose for which it was designed. It had no area or seats for spectators. The proceedings in the Senate were to be closed to the public. The first Senate, the only one to be divided into three sessions, met here for the first two sessions, in 1789 and 1790. It was the first of only five places used by the Senate in its history. Sadly, a fire destroyed this building in 1833.

In 1790, the government moved to Philadelphia. The first Congress opened its third session in the Senate chamber of Congress Hall, the new county court house, on December 6. For the next ten years the Senate enjoyed these very elegant accommodations. With the move, from the Senate chamber in New York, came the two royal portraits. Covering the floor was a new, brightly colored carpet, with an eagle holding thirteen arrows and an olive branch. Red leather chairs graced each desk. It was another room which enhanced the Senate's eminent status.

In 1800 the government moved to the new capital, Washington, D.C. For the next ten years the Senate met in small quarters on the ground floor of the new Capitol building, since the rest of the building was not yet completed. After 1810 the Senate met in the chamber located on the second floor of the north wing of the completed Capitol. In August 1814 the British burned the building and the Senate was forced to move to a small, plain residence one block away. Finally, the restoration of the destroyed Capitol was completed in 1819 and the Senate settled into its present home.

The capitol building looked then, much as it does today, except for the dome. During the Civil War the original dome, which was considerably flatter, was replaced by the soaring cast iron dome we see today. This seven million pound structure was manufactured by the Janes and Beebe Ironworks, which was then located in what is now The Bronx.

First Senate Issues

The first Congress lasted from 1789 until after the election in 1791. In that two-year period it had to take action on just about every issue that any congress in history had to confront, including: taxes, public lands, slavery, tariffs, Indian affairs, Senate salaries, sectionalism and national unity, designing a national court system, making the federal system work, paying the national and state debt and dealing with the threat of war, which, for example, should illustrate the difficult challenge facing the Senate. The treaty establishing an alliance between the United States and France in 1778 was still on the books in 1789. One provision bound the United States to help France defend their West Indies against all foes. The British fleets were already menacing French Islands. There was a great deal of sympathy for France in the country, but Washington, swayed by Hamilton, accepted the idea that war had to be avoided at all costs. Shortly after the outbreak of war between Britain and France he issued a Proclamation of Neutrality (1793).

What complicated this issue further was that for ten years Britain had refused to honor her obligations under the peace treaty ending the revolution, by retaining control of all the frontier posts on United States soil. She openly sold intoxicating beverages and firearms to the Indians and encouraged them to attack American pioneers. Furthermore, Britain had begun to divide people along the lines of those who thought like Jefferson and those who thought like Hamilton, who wanted to maintain relations with Britain. We relied on the tariffs from foreign trade to keep our government solvent, yet about seventy-five percent of it came from Britain. Jeffersonians felt obligated to fulfill our treaty promises and since France helped us in our time of need, they believed we were obligated to reciprocate. To try to resolve these outstanding problems Washington sent John Jay to Britain. The Jay Treaty which came out of the negotiations was extremely controversial and split the Senate along the Jeffersonian and Hamiltonian factions.

In addition there were problems of form which needed to be resolved. Without a precedent to follow it was necessary to devise and agree upon a method of operation or policy for many issues, such as: the use of titles, proper protocol, defining limits on presidential and congressional power. There were even many basic housekeeping tasks, such as: building lighthouses, securing federal property, organizing federal departments and journals of record, all of which had to be acted upon.

From the tug of war over where to locate the capital before the congress assembled, to the actual structure of the government, political differences existed between persons who believed that a strong central government was a necessity and those who held that the less power a government exercised, the better it would be for people. These essential beliefs and their expressions, were a recurring theme in the first Senate and will be found in the biographies of the senators. Such attitudes developed out of one's philosophy about the nature of man and from one's view of what constituted the ideal society. Two men, Alexander Hamilton and Thomas Jefferson, so personified the differences, that when members of the first Senate leaned toward one side or the other, the terms "Hamiltonian" or "Jeffersonian" described their views. Furthermore, Hamiltonians are also called federalists, seeking a strong federal government, and Jeffersonians are also called antifederalists, seeking a less powerful central/federal government. Some quotes from these men, who seem to have evolved attitudes completely opposite from their status at birth, will help to draw the political battle lines more clearly.

Alexander Hamilton was born into humble circumstances yet developed a deep distrust of the common man. He said, "All communities divide themselves into the few and the many. The first are the rich and well born; the other, the mass of people. The people are turbulent and changing; they seldom judge or determine right." Hamilton, responding to Jefferson on one occasion, said, "Your people, sir, are a great beast," and in a speech at the Constitutional Convention, "Take mankind in general, they are vicious — their passions may be operated upon... Take mankind as they are, and what are they governed by? their passions..."

Jefferson, born into the world of the privileged, landed aristocracy, became the spokesman for the opposite view, "Men... are naturally divided into two parties. Those who fear and distrust the people... (and) Those who identify themselves with the people, have confidence in them, cherish and consider them as the most honest and safe... depository of the public interest." He also said, "The mass of mankind has not been born with saddles on their backs, nor a favored few booted and spurred, ready to ride them legitimately, by the grace of God." Jefferson was a champion of the common man. He envisioned a nation where each person owned their own land, was free, independent, well educated and prepared to defend their own interests as well as respect that of others. The following quotation, however, sums up his view of democracy of, by, and for the people. "Whenever the people are well-informed, they can be trusted with their own government: whenever things get so far wrong as to attract their notice, they may be relied on to set them to rights."

On one hand, the informed masses became the foundation of Jefferson's Democratic-Republican Party. On the other, the cultivation of the commercial, financial, shipping and manufacturing interests, accompanied by a distrust of the masses, became the basis of the Federalist Party, personified by Hamilton, the first Secretary of the Treasury. He had responsibility to propose a program that would develop the financial apparatus for the new country. His financial program became the center of the political battles in the first Senate.

Hamilton wanted to build acceptance of the new nation's credit. To support the revolutionary war against England, bonds had been sold and the national debt was about $54 million; few people believed the treasury could meet this obligation. They feared that the bonds they had bought, along with the small percent of interest they were to have been paid, would be nearly worthless. They were afraid of being wiped out when the new government reneged.

Even though the government was struggling with enormous debt and undefined revenue, Hamilton wanted the Congress to fund the entire national debt at par, which meant paying off the debt at face value plus accumulated interest. It seemed to be an honest idea and the only way to build faith and trust in the new government. Those privileged to be aware of this information used the plan for personal gain. Since there was a good chance that the new government, to gain credibility, **would** adopt Hamilton's plan, these few felt comfortable enough to speculate. If these seemingly worthless bonds would actually be worth full value, plus interest, one could pocket quite a hefty sum by buying large quantities of these bonds from the fearful, and unsuspecting, general public for a mere ten or fifteen cents on the dollar, before the plan was announced publicly. Turning them in later, at full face value, would net a whopping profit. Some of the fifty-five delegates to the Constitutional Convention, and some senators, were involved in this get-rich scheme. It is not inappropriate to label this the first widespread government insider corruption scandal.

Hamilton went even further than paying off the federal obligations. He also proposed assuming the state debts, a little over $21.5 million, to further strengthen the power of the federal government. This plan was especially controversial. Some states, mostly in the north, such as Massachusetts, had heavy debts and were happy with the proposal, some had small debts, such as Rhode Island, while some, such as Virginia, had almost finished paying their debts and couldn't see the logic in being stuck with bills from someone else. This proposal tended to divide states along north-south lines and highlighted other differences.

The policies were shaped to favor the wealthier groups, thus tying them into supporting the federal administration. Hamilton felt that if the propertied classes experienced real prosperity they would have capital to invest in industry and that some of their wealth would trickle down to the masses and the federal government would flourish. Since Hamilton believed that the debt was a blessing which acted as a glue to bind the union, succeeding generations called him, "The Father of the National Debt".

The money to meet interest and principal payments were to come from tariffs (taxes) on goods coming into the country. Some of the tariffs or customs duties were designed to raise revenue and some were fixed in order to protect our infant industries from foreign competition. He thought that funding the foreign debt would encourage European trade. Some money would come from the sale of the vast federal land holdings. Finally, money would come from excise taxes, that is, taxes placed on domestic manufactured items. The best known of these was the Whisky Tax that provoked a rebellion, mostly among Pennsylvania farmers. Hamilton advocated, and Washington agreed to, the use of federal troops to crush the uprising, thus further establishing the primacy of the federal government, which was exactly what the antifederalists feared.

One of the more controversial proposals was for a privately owned national bank, which would have semi-public functions, with the government as a major stockholder. It provoked a major constitutional debate. Jefferson, the strict constructionist, maintained that if the constitution didn't specifically authorize an action, such as chartering a national bank, that it was not legal to do so. Hamilton believed in a loose construction of the Constitution. Such an interpretation held that if an action was not specifically forbidden by the Constitution, then it was legal. He maintained that the right to create a bank was implied in the last of the eighteen powers granted to congress. The crucial sentence under the powers of congress reads, "To make all laws which shall be necessary and proper for carrying into execution the foregoing powers..."

Of course, not all legislation considered by the congress concerned areas of government within Hamilton's jurisdiction. Yet these too, had an indirect effect on Hamilton's position. For example, the legislation proposed to establish a federal judiciary bolstered Hamilton's program for a strong federal government.

Federalists tended to be pro-British in their foreign policy views. Jeffersonians were inclined to be pro-French and more open to the changes taking place in the world during the time of the French Revolution.

Issues of protocol and the use of titles separated the two factions as well. Hamiltonians/Federalists tended to be more formal, more traditional and hierarchical. Jeffersonians favored democratic simplicity and forms which promoted equality.

Since the Senate debates were closed to the public we must turn to the official, constitutionally mandated, *Congressional Record*, for information about the proceedings of the meetings. While that offers one view of the workings of the first Senate, it cannot be the same as being there. The closest we can now come to having been a fly on the wall of the Senate chamber is one man's diary. Much of the information about the operation of, and the personalities involved, comes to us from the private journal of Senator William Maclay from Pennsylvania. His diary provides us with a unique and interesting description of the debates, the opinions, the foibles and the functioning of these formative meetings. However, he was not just an observer, he was one of the players.

George H. Haynes, in his book on the United States Senate, written in 1938, quotes J. Franklin Jameson, noted historian, about Senator Maclay's personality and reliability as an observer:

"...for much took place behind the closed doors of the Senate chamber during the first Congress we have no other ample record except that of this atrabilious and parvanimous[2] creature.... Most readers think that because Maclay says that men acted thus and so, they actually did. All things look yellow to the jaundiced eye. Everything this contemptible creature set down is poisoned and distorted by his mean malignancy. He was a man of bitterest prejudices.." To Maclay, Hamilton was a "damnable villain," the machination of whose "gladiators" and "hired partisans" he thought he detected at many a critical juncture in the senate ....

This extremely critical view of Maclay reflects the author's bias against populist views and is not a balanced judgment. Anyone who wishes to understand the workings of the first Senate must read and use Maclay's journal.

Many such personality differences and seriously complex matters were dealt with in ways that somehow held the Senate and the nation together enough to give the new government a chance to survive. In the process, the traditions, the precedents, and the structures which delineated the senatorial role for the succeeding 200 years were all established by the men who served in that first Senate.

Biographical Sketches of the First United States Senators

CONNECTICUT

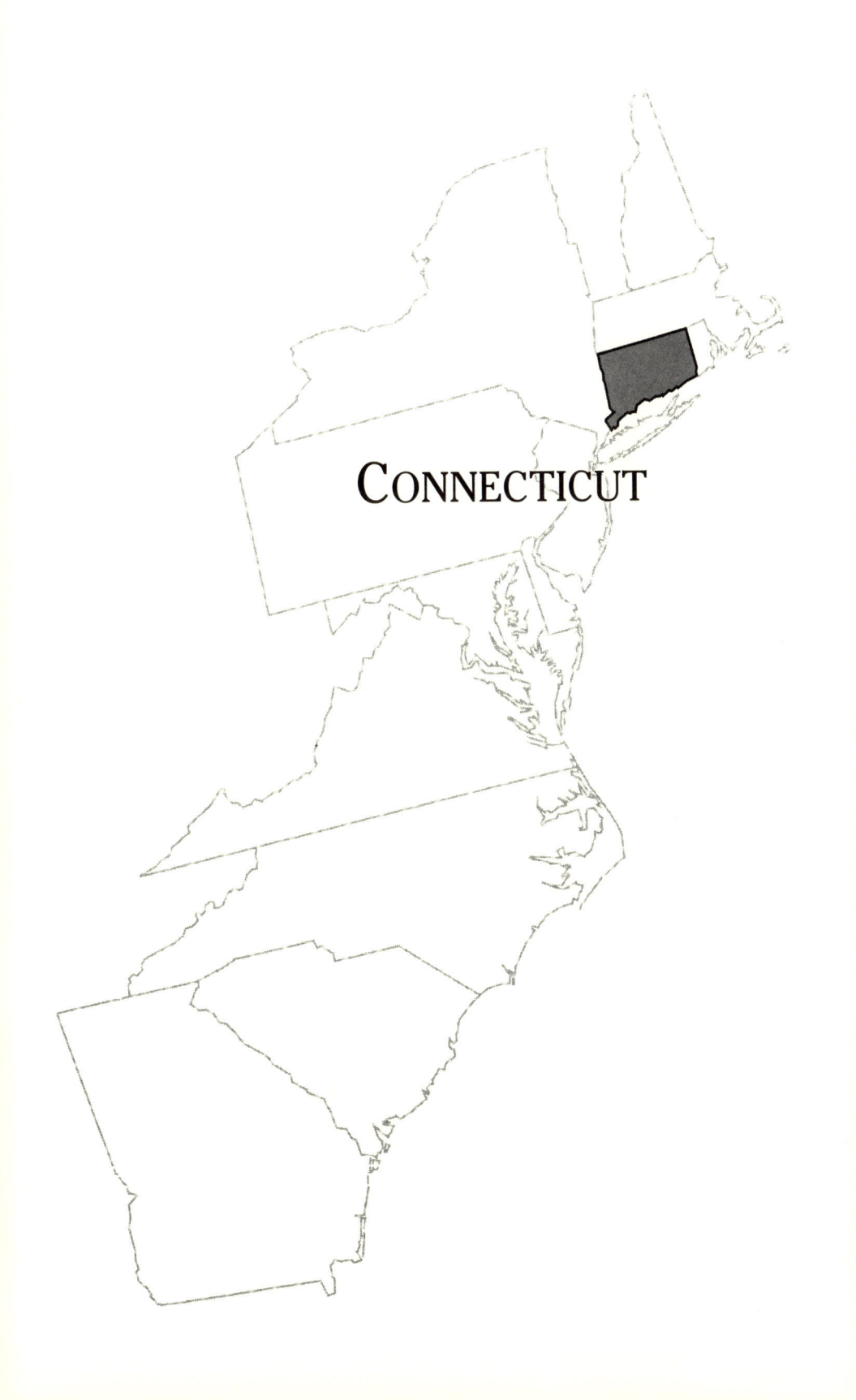

OLIVER ELLSWORTH
April 29, 1745 *November 26, 1807*

Near the end of his life, Oliver Ellsworth said he thought he was without imagination, but rated high for strength of reason, wisdom and good sense in public affairs. He thought he was moderate in temper and general ability. Others said he was tall, dignified, commanding, particular in appearance and a brilliant conversationalist, but that he talked to himself even when others were around. He was conservative by nature and moderate in all things except snuff, to which he was addicted. This is one picture of the man but it is incomplete.

Oliver Ellsworth was born to a comfortable, but not wealthy, family. At seventeen he entered Yale College. This institution had been founded as Collegiate School at Killingworth, Connecticut in 1701. It moved to New Haven in 1716 and took the name Yale College when Elihu Yale, an English benefactor, gave a very generous sum for its expansion.

After two years at Yale, for personal reasons, he and a friend left and went to the College of New Jersey, in Princeton. Originally chartered as the College of New Jersey in 1746 it opened in Elizabeth in 1747, moved to Newark in 1749 and finally to Princeton in 1756, where it remains to this day. The name would be changed officially to Princeton University, in 1896.

Ellsworth received a B.A. from the College of New Jersey. Though he was attracted to law, to please his father he prepared for the religious life. Before long he changed back to law and his father cut off his financial support. To pay his bills, while studying law, Ellsworth taught school. He passed the bar in 1771. A year later he married Abigail Wolcott. In addition to his work as a lawyer he cut and sold lumber to pay his debts. He was too poor to afford a horse, so when the Hartford court was in session he had to walk the ten miles each way.

Following his success in a case that drew much publicity, he was appointed Attorney General for the colony. His income and fame grew after 1775 and he was recognized as a leader of the Connecticut bar.

In 1775 he was elected to the General Assembly and two years later to the Continental Congress where he served for six years. Concurrently he was appointed to the governor's council which became the Supreme Court of Errors. From 1784 until 1789, he remained a judge of that court.

After the Battle of Lexington and Concord, Ellsworth was appointed one of five Connecticut commissioners to supervise the state's war expenditures, and was appointed to the State Council of Safety which controlled military measures. He was a hard worker, completely reliable and very competent.

In 1787 he was a delegate to the Constitutional Convention. There he proposed using the phrase "the government of the United States," which became standard. He was a staunch advocate of equal state representation and of states' rights. He believed that the decision should be left to the states, of whether or not to stop the importation of slaves and to end slavery. He voted for the three-fifths compromise that counted slaves for taxes and representation. Finally, he was opposed to a federal salary for Congress and moved that payment be made by state governments. Though active in many sessions, he did not sign the final Constitution.

Connecticut's ratification convention had the benefit of his experience. He worked hard for the adoption of the Constitution. His *Letters of a Landholder* contained his reasoned arguments for its adoption and were influential in developing support for ratification. As a result, he was rewarded with election to the first Senate.

His contributions to the work of the first Senate were also quite significant. He reported the first set of Senate rules and guided them to adoption. With others he worked on plans to print the required journal; reported for the conference committee that worked on the Bill of Rights; and wrote the measure that admitted North Carolina into the Union. He wrote the bill which organized the federal judiciary, and the one establishing a government for the Ohio territory. He also wrote regulations for the new consular service.

He authored the Non-Intercourse Act which threatened Rhode Island with trade restrictions. This measure helped to persuade that state to ratify the Constitution. While objecting to some details, he supported Hamilton's plan for assuming the state debts, supported the bill for a national bank, and the Whisky Tax. Ellsworth is given credit for getting the controversial Jay Treaty with England passed in the Senate.

He enjoyed enormous respect in the Senate and wielded power through the force of his personality and his legal wisdom. Ellsworth drew the two-year term in the division of the first Senate. He was reelected in 1791, but resigned before his term was up, in 1796, to become Chief Justice of the United States. He accepted the appointment to the court with great modesty, for he knew his own shortcomings, and the inadequacy of his training and preparation.

In February 1799 he was sent to France as an envoy extraordinary. The four months trip permanently affected Ellsworth's health. He was not well enough to sail home. His son carried the letter of resignation as Chief Justice, to the president. The following March he left for home and for retirement.

He remained active in Congregational church affairs into retirement. He studied theology and pursued his interest in agriculture as well, publishing several articles about practical farming. In 1790, the degree of LL.D. was awarded him by Yale, followed in 1797, by both Dartmouth and Princeton.

His death was marked by memorials throughout the nation. He was buried in the old cemetery in Windsor, Connecticut.

WILLIAM SAMUEL JOHNSON
October 7, 1727 *November 14, 1818*

    William Samuel Johnson was born into a prominent family. His mother was both the daughter of, and the widow of, politically important large land owners. His father, a well-known Anglican clergyman and philosopher, was the first president of King's College. Chartered by King George II, in 1754, the college was located in a school room in the vestry of Trinity Church in New York City. In 1760 it moved a few blocks north into its own quarters, where it grew slowly until 1776 when the New York Committee of Safety requisitioned the building and suspended classes for the duration of the Revolution. It was reopened by the State Legislature with control vested in the Regents of the State University of New York. The name was changed to Columbia College and reverted to private auspices in 1787. Two more moves brought it to its present site on the upper west side of Manhattan, in 1897. It was recognized as Columbia University by New York

State in 1912. The history of the college and the Johnson family remain closely connected for two generations.

It is no surprise that William's father had him studying his primer at age four, reading his Psalter and Catechism at five and reading such classics as Aesop and Virgil, in translation, at eight. Johnson entered Yale at thirteen and graduated in 1744. He then studied at Harvard where in three years he received his M.A. at the age of twenty. His father encouraged him to prepare for a religious career and for a short time he was a lay reader, but he developed an overriding interest in the law. He began studying law and, without formal training, started to practice. Many of his earliest cases were concerned with religious disputes in New York and Connecticut and these brought him favorable publicity.

From 1753, when he started his public life, he served variously as an ensign in a militia company, a member of the colony's house of representatives in 1761 and in 1765, and a representative in the upper chamber from 1766 until 1775. Because of his pleasing personality and conciliatory manner, Johnson was the first Episcopalian to be brought into that body.

Johnson's inheritance, his friends, professional acquaintances, social position and all his family connections worked to keep him in opposition to the break with the English Crown. His wife, Anne Beach, was an outspoken loyalist. By nature and training Johnson was very cautious and always sought to compromise. This conservative approach guided his actions through the revolutionary period and caused him considerable political and legal difficulty with the more revolutionary forces that held sway after 1774.

From 1767 to 1771, Johnson was Connecticut's colonial agent in London. There he developed powerful social and political connections and was awarded an honorary doctorate from Oxford. He met many churchmen and literary figures and developed a lifelong friendship with his namesake, Dr. Samuel Johnson. In spite of these connections he continued to oppose the Stamp Act and took an active part in the Stamp Act Congress. He supported the non-importation agreements and actively opposed the Townshend duties, those taxes levied on glass, white lead, paper and tea, but tried to balance his position by criticism of the more radical opposition leaders. While in London he won two important cases for Connecticut, and considerable notoriety.

Johnson was appointed a judge of the Connecticut Superior Court in 1771 but, within a year, felt compelled to resign since he was openly opposed to the independence forces who were in the majority. His attempt to secure an appointment from the Crown at the same time received critical publicity but, in spite of the controversy, his personal popularity remained undiminished and he was elected to the first Continental Congress. Sensing that the radicals would widen the breech with England he declined the position. After the battle of Lexington and Concord, the Governor of Connecticut sent Johnson to arrange a cease-fire with General Gage, who had been appointed Governor of Massachusetts. The more radical elements did not want to cool the revolutionary ardor generated by action at Lexington and Concord and the pro-British faction were critical because he had not succeeded in his attempt to get a cease-fire. Though the effort was unsuccessful, Johnson was strongly criticized and was dropped from the Governor's council. He then resumed his law practice.

His political life had a turning point in 1779. Johnson, always the compromiser, sought relief for the coastal communities. When he foolishly agreed to meet with the British commanders raiding the area, the Revolutionary forces arrested him. He denied any contact or improper intent and after he took an oath of fidelity Governor Trumbull exonerated him. He immediately stopped all fence straddling and moved in harmony with the revolutionary forces. He was elected to the Confederation Congress in 1784, where he served for three years.

In 1787 he was appointed president of Columbia College, his father's old position, and held that post until retirement in 1799. Under his leadership the school grew in the number of its offerings, in the size of the professional staff and in its income and endowment.

In that same year Johnson was also appointed head of the five delegates sent to the Constitutional Convention from Connecticut. He did not miss a single day, from arrival until adjournment. He favored the extension of federal authority and held that there could not be treason against a state because sovereignty resided in the Union. He opposed *ex post facto* laws because they implied suspicion of the national legislature. From the beginning he favored a two-house legislature, especially a separate Senate. He argued that the judicial power had to extend to questions of "law and equity," and the phrase itself was adopted on his motion. After the convention he worked for adoption of the constitution, stressing that the new system was a federal one, forming one nation out of the many states. He argued that law was the only force this new government would employ and that it would operate only upon individuals who failed in their duty to their country.

In 1789 he was elected to the Senate. He was a firm supporter of all Hamilton's measures, except the idea that the president had the power to remove officers once approved by the Senate. His most noteworthy contribution was in shaping the Judiciary Act of 1789. The decision to move the capital to Philadelphia forced him to resign, for he would have been too far from his college duties in New York and from his home in Connecticut.

Senator Maclay of Pennsylvania did not share Johnson's enthusiasm for English jurisprudence and other things English. He noted that, although Johnson lived in New York, he accepted pay for constant travel back and forth to his regular home in Connecticut. Georgia delegate William Pierce said, "Johnson possesses the manners of a gentleman and a sweet temper, an affectionate style of address and an eloquent and clear oratorical style."

Though Johnson was very religious and involved with intellectual matters, he was quite worldly when it came to the accumulation of wealth. He acquired a sizable fortune from his inheritance, his legal practice and from his investments. He invested heavily in securities such as those funding the debt of the United States. As president of Columbia College he spent much time in New York City, but maintained his Connecticut residence and social connections.

In 1799, when he resigned from Columbia College, he returned to his Connecticut home where his days were spent giving advice on law, politics, theology, and literature. His long life ended at age nine-two. He was buried in the Episcopal cemetery in Stratford.

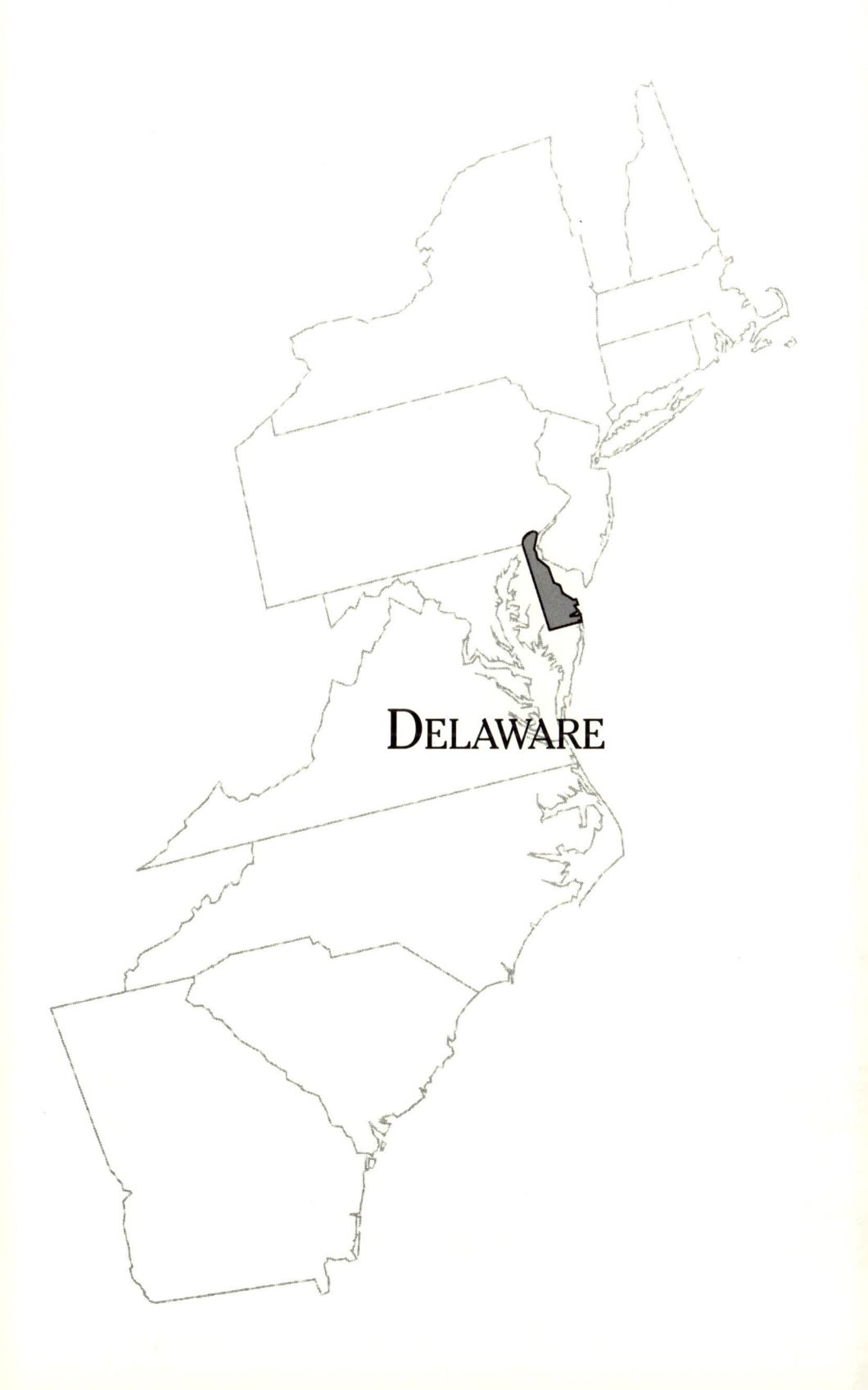

Delaware

RICHARD BASSETT

April 2, 1745 *September 15, 1815*

While Richard was still very young his father, a tavern keeper, abandoned his wife who died soon after. Richard was adopted by a relative named Peter Lawson, of Maryland, who lived on an estate called Bohemia Manor. Richard Bassett, well schooled, eventually became a lawyer. When Lawson died, Bassett inherited the estate. Along with earnings from his law practice, this made Bassett a wealthy man. When he turned twenty-one he moved to Delaware, where he married Ann Ennalls. They had a daughter, Ann, and adopted another daughter named Rachel. He and his wife divorced. He later married a Miss Bruff.

Bassett was converted to Methodism by George Whitefield and he never lost his fervor. He did much to promote the spread of his new faith, generously using his wealth to do so.

At the time of the Revolution he had a solid reputation in his state as a skillful lawyer. He was without public experience until he became a captain in the Dover Light Horse and fought in the New Jersey Campaigns of 1777.

Following the revolution he served on the state council of safety and for ten years was a member of the governor's council. Bassett represented Delaware at the Annapolis Convention and was sent to the Constitutional Convention the next year, where he appears to have made little contribution.

Perhaps he was intimidated by the wealthy and knowledgeable men about him, or perhaps, he just wanted to listen and learn. Learn he did, for in 1792 he was appointed to the committee to write a new Delaware constitution and he made many practical contributions. Upon his return from Philadelphia he was a delegate to the Delaware ratifying convention, the first to approve the new federal Constitution.

Delaware sent him to the first Senate where he voted against assuming the state debts and for locating the capital along the Potomac. On all other issues he supported the Hamiltonian position, including the president's removal power over all appointments.

From September 1793, to January 1799, he was Chief Justice of the Court of Common Pleas for Delaware. In 1797 he was a presidential elector and voted for John Adams. The years from 1799 to 1801, when he was governor of his state, were placid. His administration, while not active or exciting, was honorable. Finally, he was one of the midnight judges appointed by John Adams in the attempt to keep the federal judiciary in Federalist hands after Jefferson's election.

Bassett had good common sense and was always willing to compromise on difficult issues. He was not imaginative, nor did he exhibit any real leadership qualities. He was likable, but not politically important.

Bassett died at age seventy, at Bohemia Manor, and was buried in the Wilmington and Brandywine cemetery.

GEORGE READ

September 18, 1733   *September 21, 1798*

    George Read had the distinction of signing both the Declaration of Independence and the United States Constitution, as well as serving as a member of the first Senate, one of only two men to do so. His father, John Read, and his mother, Mary Howell, came from the large landholder-planter class. At an early age George was sent to the academy of Rev. Francis Alison in New London, Pennsylvania. At fifteen he finished his studies and became an apprentice in the law office of John Moland, in Philadelphia. Soon after opening his practice he developed an excellent reputation for legal expertise, for solid organization of argumentation and for calmness under fire. He was rigid in application of legal ethics and truthfulness, and was called the "honest lawyer." Read was tall and slim in build, with very fine features and, with his careful attention to dress, he made an attractive figure. His practice required him to move through much of Delaware and the southern counties of Maryland, and he became well known in the region.

In 1763 he married the widow Gertrude Ross Till, who had a daughter and three sons. The union produced one son; thus, Read had responsibility for a sizable family by the age of thirty. In that same year he became Attorney General of Delaware, where he remained for eleven years.

He protested the Stamp Act, saying that if any measures bringing revenue to Great Britain by internal taxes were enforced, the colonists would become slaves. It would be a mistake to consider Read a revolutionary, however, as he was basically conservative. He viewed Britain's moves as disturbing the status quo and was anxious to defend traditional colonial rights. He always sought compromise in order to avoid a break. He chose his words with great care and selected the protests he supported.

For twelve years he served in the provincial assembly. There he won endorsement for the Non-Importation Agreements and for relief measures for Boston after the Intolerable Acts were passed in 1774. Though he was a member of the first and second Continental Congresses until 1777, he attended irregularly.

The resolution for independence on July 2, 1776, did not win his vote, probably because the majority sentiment in Delaware was Tory. When Jefferson's Declaration was engrossed, however, he signed the document. George Read was one of the four men in the first Senate who signed the Declaration of Independence.

As presiding officer of Delaware's Constitutional Convention in 1776, Read was, by far, the most influential member. He may have been the sole author of the state's revolutionary constitution. As speaker of the legislative council, he became vice-president of the state. When the British captured state President McKinly, Read became the chief executive officer. He was indefatigable in efforts to raise money, troops, and provisions for the revolutionary army. He is credited with turning the sentiment in Delaware toward support for independence. Between 1772 and 1778 he sat in the legislative assembly. He asked to be relieved of his duties at the end of March 1778 but the people of Delaware continued him in public life.

In 1782, the Confederation Congress elected him the Judge of the Court of Appeals in admiralty cases, which position he held while pursuing his private legal practice. In 1784, New York and Massachusetts appointed him one of nine commissioners to adjust conflicting land claims.

Read was a representative to the Annapolis convention and to the Constitutional Convention where he championed small states' interests. He wanted separate legislative branches and equal representation for all states. He feared the larger states, but never worried about too much power in the hands of the federal government. Largely through his efforts, Delaware was the first state to ratify the Constitution.

He was elected to the first Senate where he drew the two-year seat. He was reelected in 1791. As usual, he was not regular in attendance, but was predictable with his vote. He supported assumption of state debts, the national bank, all Hamilton's financial plans, and the president's power to remove officers. He opposed any move to open Senate sessions to the public. Read did not play a leadership role, and was quite ordinary in his talents.

He resigned his Senate seat in September 1793, to become Chief Justice of Delaware. He kept that post until his death in New Castle, at age sixty-five. He was buried in Immanuel cemetery in that city.

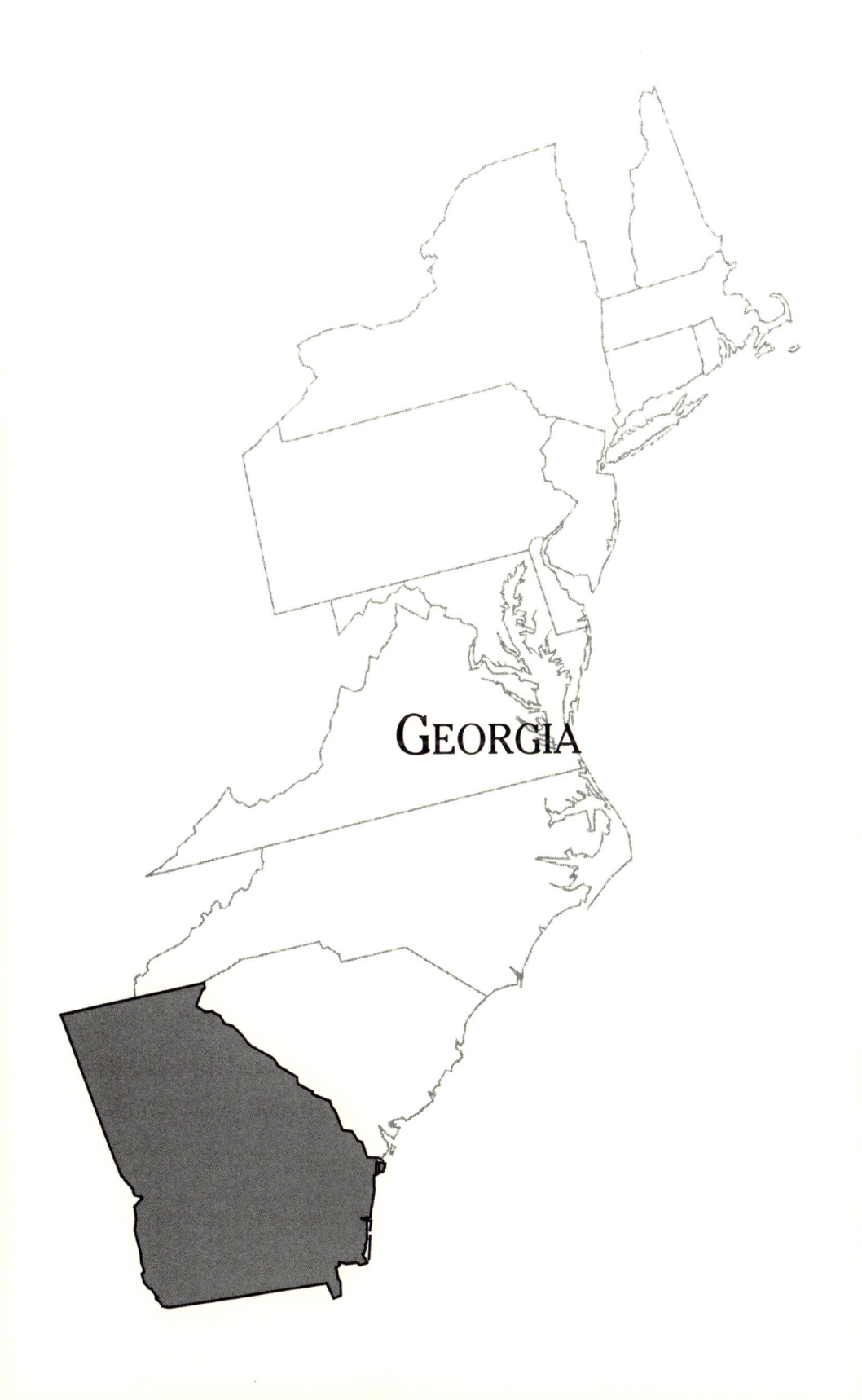

Georgia

WILLIAM FEW

June 8, 1748   *July 16, 1828*

    In 1759, when William Few's father could no longer make a living as a tobacco farmer in the Baltimore area, he moved the family to Orange County, North Carolina near the present city of Durham. Everyone in the family, including eleven-year old William, had to work long hours developing the new farm. He spent less than a year in school and received his education through reading and from itinerant teachers. He was raised as a Methodist and learned to value hard work, thrift and simple living.

    The Few family, like all other interior settlers in Carolina, found that land prices were very high, interest rates were exorbitant, and all necessary legal services for land transactions and deed recording were costly. Worst of all, interior defenses were totally inadequate. They properly blamed the coastal elites for these problems. The fourth and fifth generation British coastal settlers were comfortable and well-off by this time in our history. They speculated in western lands and profited from high interest and high prices. They controlled the government and courts, and benefitted from legal fees. They intended to keep it that way. Furthermore, they didn't want to spend their money providing a defense for the newcomers. These serious differences between the haves and the have-nots resulted in a series of uprisings against the coastal elite and the British rulers. These uprisings, were referred to as the Regulator War.

The Few family was involved in the Regulator War (1765-1771), during which the British destroyed their farm and summarily hanged his brother, James. Because his father had posted bond for several Regulator outlaws, and was thus involved in complicated legal and financial difficulties, he moved the family to a Quaker settlement in St. Paul's Parish, Georgia, in 1775. William, twenty-seven years old, stayed behind to handle the legal affairs. During this period, he married Catherine Nicholsen, daughter of the well known and well-off Commodore Nicholsen.

While serving as a lieutenant colonel during the revolution, William also served as a member of both the Georgia general assembly and the executive council of the state. He was appointed commissioner of Indians and state surveyor general, and was sent to the Continental Congress twice. Few studied law on his own, was admitted to the bar, and in 1776, began his practice.

He was one of six Georgia delegates sent to the Constitutional Convention, in Philadelphia, in 1787. He stayed throughout the deliberations and signed the document. His contributions were not noteworthy. He was a rough-and-ready kind of man, lacking the polish so characteristic of other delegates.

He was a member of the state ratifying convention, working hard to secure Georgia's approval of the new government. His work was recognized when he was elected to the first Senate, where he drew a four-year term.

He played a curious role in the Senate. He voted to keep New York as the national capital which put him at odds with all other southern delegates. He voted for a tariff rate that was against the interests of his own state, and he always voted for military bills while assuring the Senate that Georgia was secure and needed no federal help.

The following information sheds some light on his positions. In 1789, the Georgia legislature authorized the sale of 25.5 million acres to several land companies owned by New York City banks. Since the land belonged to the Indians, this seizure and sale caused a great deal of unrest in the Indian community.

Investigations revealed that just about every legislator, many other state officials, and the two federal senators were bribed with stock in the companies, or were involved in some fraudulent way with this action. Public knowledge of the scandal did not spread until several court cases shed light on the secret arrangements after 1798. Few, along with his fellow Senator, James Gunn, was implicated in that scandal.

Senator Maclay, of Pennsylvania noted that Few was a lawyer, but clearly didn't understand technical details about the Naturalization Bill. He also reported that Few said some very improper things, and discoursed on a very low level. In light of subsequent developments, it seems clear that he was working for his personal interests and not for those of his state. Few chose not to run again, but did agree to serve another term in the state general assembly. In 1796, he was appointed a judge of the judicial circuit of Georgia, and served until 1799.

By this time, the senator's role in the land grab scandal was common knowledge and voter anger was growing. Motivated by the reaction of voters, Few decided, in the summer of 1799, to move to New York City.

In short order, he was elected to the New York assembly where he served for four years. Then, in quick succession, he was appointed inspector of state prisons and commissioner of loans. He was elected a city alderman and finally mayor of the city of New York. In 1804, he was appointed director of the Bank of the Manhattan Company, one of the most important financial institutions in the country at that time, and held that post for ten years. Finally he was chosen president of the City Bank, and finished his career in that position.

He died at the home of his son-in-law at Fishkill-on-the-Hudson, survived by his wife and three daughters. He was buried in the Dutch Reformed Church cemetery in Beacon, New York.

JAMES GUNN

March ?, 1739 *July 30, 1801*

James Gunn has fewer lines in standard references than any other prominent figure in early American history. Furthermore, there are discrepancies in the limited biographical sketches that are available. We know that he was born in Virginia in 1739, but nothing is known about his childhood, other than that he was educated in the common schools and after an apprenticeship was admitted to the practice of law. When Gunn moved to Savannah, Georgia, and began to practice, there was little legal competition, since settlement in Georgia had only begun in 1733. Within a short time, he had all the work he could handle.

He was an active patriot during the revolution and even after the war when the Loyalists continued the war for control. It was particularly savage in Georgia and South Carolina. He was also in the battle to relieve Savannah in 1782, following which he returned to his law practice. He remained active in the Georgia militia. He rose rapidly through the ranks to colonel and within a few years to Brigadier General of the state militia. Although he was elected to the Confederation Congress, he did not serve.

With this very limited service and experience, he was elected to represent Georgia in the first United States Senate, where his record was undistinguished. He drew the six-year position in the lottery, and was reelected in 1795. This election took place before the scandalous land grab became common knowledge, which resulted in the popular rebellion that threw many of the rascals out of office. Thus, Gunn escaped the voter's vengeance. There were violent Indian reactions to the land grab, and this caused much Senate concern. Gunn contradicted all reports of unrest, and assured the Senate that the Indians were peaceful and accepting, and that no action was required of the Senate. His vote for postponement of a Senate study, and his assurances that there was no improper action between the state of Georgia and the Creek Indians, resulted in blocking any Senate action to correct the unjust and illegal land seizure. Gunn's second Senate term expired in March 1801, and he never sought election to public office again.

He died suddenly in Louisville, Georgia. His body lies in the cemetery of the Old Capitol, in Louisville, which served as the first state capitol from 1796 to 1806, before Atlanta became the capitol.

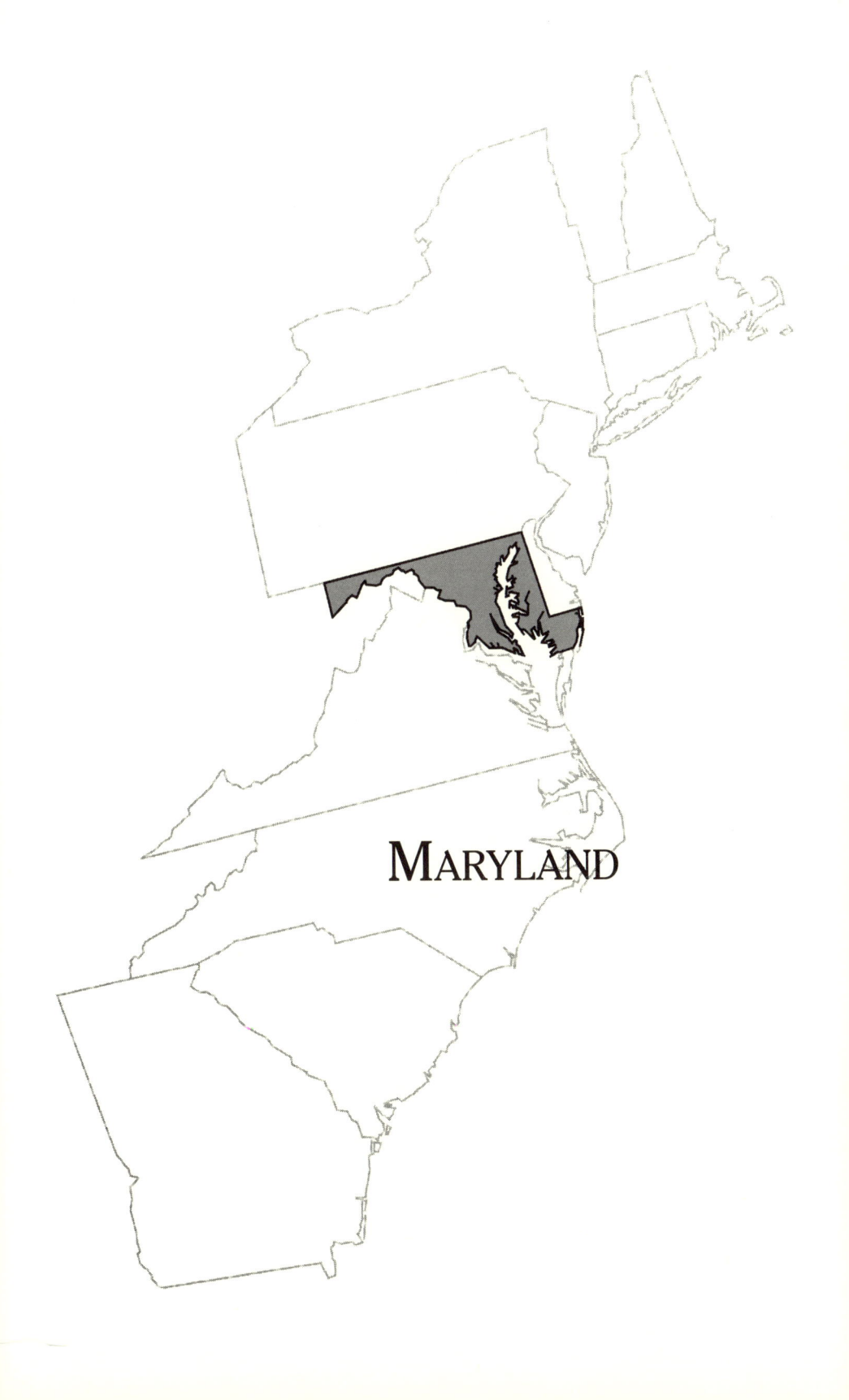

MARYLAND

CHARLES CARROLL OF CARROLLTON
September 19, 1737 *November 14, 1832*

Charles Carroll of Carrollton played a major role in revolutionary American history. He began using "of Carrollton" in 1765 to distinguish himself from his father and cousins who had the same name, and who were also prominent public figures.

He was exceptionally well educated and well traveled. For his first eleven years as a student he attended Bohemian Manor, then, for nine years, he studied modern classics with the Jesuits at St. Omer's school in Flanders. Next he studied mathematics and metaphysics at Rheims and the College of Louis le Grand in Paris. Finally, from 1757 to 1762, he pursued law at the Inner Temple in London. After fulfilling the required five years and with the best legal preparation available at the time, he was ready to return to his native land and live the comfortable life into which he was born. He married his cousin, Mary Darnall, in 1768, and for the next five years led the life of a country gentleman. His father gave him a ten-thousand acre tract of land called Carrollton Manor.

Carroll was first activated by the fight against the Stamp Act. He believed that Britain used the colonies to enrich herself and was not concerned with colonial welfare. Upon repeal of the act Carroll publicly predicted that the fight was not over. The passage of the tea tax added to the tension in Maryland, and when the first tea ship arrived in Chesapeake Bay, Carroll advised setting fire to the vessel. That is exactly what was done.

Over the next twenty years, he held many offices. As a member of the revolutionary convention in Maryland in 1775, he was instrumental in gaining support for independence. He was elected to the Continental Congress in 1776 and 1777. He signed the Declaration of Independence, served on the important Board of War, and was on the committee sent to convince Canada to join the struggle against Britain. He was widely understood to be the Catholic spokesman for the revolution. In 1787, he was selected to represent Maryland in the Constitutional Convention, but did not serve. Until 1789, he served as a state senator.

He worked diligently for ratification of the Constitution and was rewarded with election to the first Senate. He drew a four-year term, but resigned in 1792, when he was once more elected to the state senate. While in the Senate, Carroll voted the full Hamilton financial program, with but one exception. He believed that tariffs should be so structured that they would help nations, particularly France, that helped us in the revolution. His efforts were not successful.

Senator Maclay of Pennsylvania, believing Carroll to be the richest man in the Union, was surprised when Carroll joined him against high salaries and against support for extravagant living, and when he fought against the use of all titles. Carroll also proposed wearing black crepe for a month to honor Franklin after his death. The more conservative members of the Senate were opposed. Maclay forgave Carroll for the times he voted in opposition to him because he judged him "the just man."

In 1801, he finished his last term in the Maryland Senate, and retired from public service. Twenty-five years later, he took a position as director of the newly formed Baltimore and Ohio Railroad, which laid the first twelve miles of track between Washington, D.C., and Baltimore.

Shortly thereafter, in Baltimore, the last surviving signer of the Declaration of Independence died at age ninety-five. He was buried in the Chapel of Doughoregan Manor near Ellicott City, Maryland.

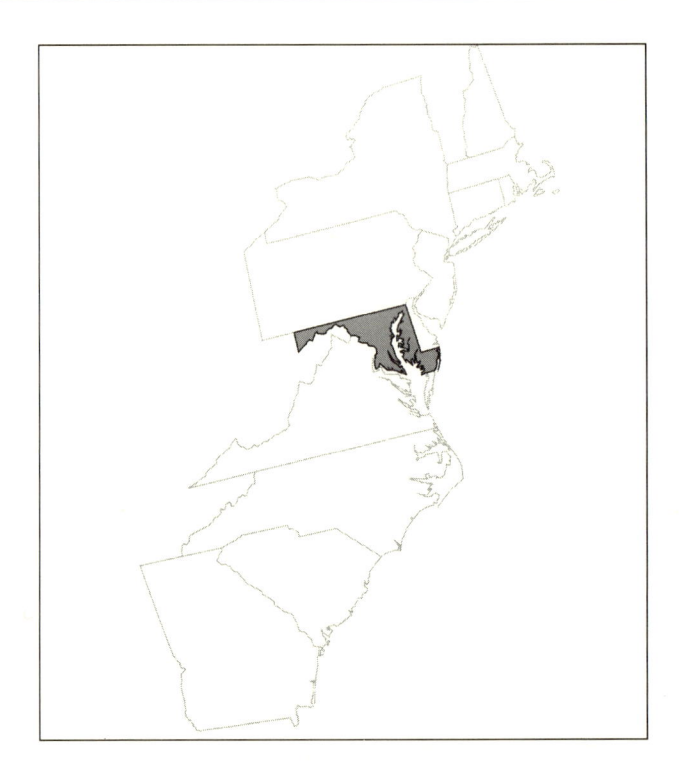

JOHN HENRY

November 7, 1750   *December 16, 1798*

John Henry was born at Weston, his family's Maryland homestead. He attended Nottingham Academy and the College of New Jersey,[3] graduating in 1769. He spent the next six years at the Middle Temple, in London, studying law. While there, he was a member of the Robin Hood Club, a popular debating society, where he defended the colonies and their protests over the Stamp Act, the tea tax, and the Intolerable Acts. Upon returning from England in 1775, he was admitted to the bar and opened a law office. At age thirty-seven he married Margaret Campbell and in the next three years they had two sons.

In 1776 he was elected to the Maryland assembly and in 1777 to the Continental Congress. Except for the three years he served in the Maryland Senate, he served in the Congress until 1787. He was vigorous in his efforts to provide for the revolutionary army. He criticized his state's efforts in support of the war and the high prices charged for army supplies. He served on committees that procured flour, obtained aid and supplies from France, and found ways to raise revenue. He also voted for making new states out of western territory. While in the Maryland Senate he voted to adopt the Articles of Confederation. His colleagues recognized him as a man of great integrity and one with the courage of his convictions.

After the adoption of the federal Constitution by Maryland, Henry was elected to the first Senate. He took his seat on April 20, 1789, drew the six-year term and was reelected in 1795. Henry was willing to give unlimited power to the federal government. He predicted that power would be consolidated at the federal level, but for this to come about, the Senate, representing the states, would have to be destroyed. He voted to give the president the power to remove officers, accepting the view that anything was implicit in the Constitution. However, he joined Senator Maclay of Pennsylvania in the fight against titles. When the Maryland legislature instructed him to vote for open sessions for the Senate, he ignored the instructions and voted to keep the sessions secret. In November 1797, the Maryland assembly elected him governor of the state. He resigned from the Senate, returned home, served one term of a year, and then retired in poor health.

Within the month he died, at age forty-eight, on his Nanticoke river estate. He was buried in the Christ Protestant Church cemetery in Cambridge, Maryland.

Massachusetts

TRISTRAM DALTON

May 28, 1738   *May 30, 1817*

    Tristram Dalton was born in Newbury, Massachusetts, to wealthy parents. He was educated in Samuel Moody's private academy, in York, then attended Harvard College in 1751, graduating in 1755. After preparing for law in Salem, he joined his father in business. By 1760, he was active in public affairs and beginning to make a name for himself. He developed a lifelong interest in education and in the public schools.

    At the time of the Intolerable Acts, in 1774, he was a delegate to the provincial congress and two years later was elected a representative to the general court. He was consistent and ardent in his support of the continental government during the revolution, but did not take part in any military or revolutionary action.

    From 1782 to 1785, he served in the state House of Representatives where he became politically powerful and well-known statewide. He was then sent to the state senate where he served for three years, from 1786 through 1788. Newbury sent him to the constitutional convention where he worked hard and effectively for ratification. After long and protracted negotiations in the Massachusetts legislature, Dalton won election to a seat in the first Senate. He drew the two-year term.

In the early and crucial issues, Dalton did not always cast his vote according to the lines of party or ideology, but appeared to deal with each issue on its own. Though he was generally supportive of the federalist program, he voted against the use of titles. He spoke long and tediously about various taxes on imports, generally on the side of the New England Federalists with a pro-British orientation; he argued so long and so vigorously to exempt some Massachusetts ports from paying revenue, that Senator Maclay thought that he had some private interest or wanted to facilitate smuggling. On most other questions, he favored the Federalist position, including a vote for the presidential power to remove officers. He failed to make any significant mark or contribution and was, in every other way, predictable and unimaginative.

When the first Senate ended on March 3, 1791, it was the last day for both Maclay and Dalton, since they had not been reelected. Maclay, a curmudgeonly, independent, outspoken character there, had not made any friends. Of all those in the Senate, only Dalton had the grace to approach Maclay, wish him well, and express best wishes for his future.

Though politically undistinguished, Dalton was considered a scholarly gentleman with significant personal accomplishments to his credit. He was accepted socially, and even admired by his colleagues. At his estate, Spring Hill, he entertained prominent figures, including; Adams, Monroe, Talleyrand, and even Washington, with whom he felt close enough to share information about his personal finances. Acting on a tip, Dalton sold most of his property in Massachusetts and invested everything in real estate in Washington, D.C. The investments failed to perform as Washington predicted. Dalton, late in life, suddenly became a poor man. As a result, he had to seek employment when he left the Senate. Through political friends, he secured an appointment as surveyor for the port of Boston, and held this position for two years.

He died in Boston. Interment was in the churchyard of St. Paul's Episcopal Church in Newburyport, Massachusetts.

CALEB STRONG

January 9, 1745   *November 7, 1819*

    Caleb Strong's father was a simple tanner, but his mother came from a prominent and well-to-do family. His basic education was provided at Reverend Samuel Moody's private academy, in York. He then attended Harvard College, graduating with highest honors in 1764. While at school, he contracted smallpox, and suffered permanent eye damage. In spite of that handicap, he studied law with Joseph Hawley, and was admitted to the bar in 1772. Strong married Sarah Hooker, daughter of the Reverend John Hooker, in 1777. They had nine children, six of whom survived infancy.

    During the next twenty years he always held at least two positions simultaneously. In 1772 he was chosen selectman for his town and until 1783 he was active on the town's committee of public safety. In 1776, he sat on the general court, a position he held for the next twenty-four years. He was on the drafting committee which wrote the state's revolutionary constitution in 1779.

In 1780, he was on the last Massachusetts council to wield executive power under the pre-revolutionary constitution. In that year, he chose to become a state senator, rather than a delegate to the Continental Congress, and he held that office for the next eight years. Recognition of his legal skills was so widespread that he was offered a position on the state's supreme court in 1783. He declined because it did not provide enough income.

At age forty-two, in 1787, he became a delegate to the Constitutional Convention, where he played an important role. He wanted a strong executive and supported a stronger union, but felt that town meeting principles were more democratic. His raised substantial arguments against the electoral college method of electing the president, but it was approved anyway. He believed that the Congress should elect the president. He favored annual elections for representatives, to keep them responsive to the people, and he wanted one method of election for both houses of Congress. While he supported the right of the House of Representatives to originate money bills, he thought the Senate should have the right to amend them. He was reluctant to support equal representation in the Senate, since he believed that the size and wealth of the state should be taken into account. He supported Maclay's position for low federal salaries.

He had to leave Philadelphia in August because of his wife's illness and thus did not sign the Constitution. He joined other Federalists in Massachusetts working for ratification. Largely as a result of his work at the convention, he became one of the first two Senators from his state. He drew the four-year term, was reelected in 1793, but resigned in 1796 to return to private practice. In the Senate, he consistently supported Hamilton's policies. To him fell the task of presenting and defending Hamilton's plan for a national bank. Much of the credit for the Judiciary Act, and the organization of the judiciary, must go to him. He was persuasive in argument and careful in legal detail, making his work on the judiciary probably his greatest contribution to the new nation. He became famous in these years, for he was often in the midst of controversy. When Washington needed approval for John Jay's mission to England, it was Strong who provided firm support until the controversial treaty was finally ratified.[4]

Strong became Federalist Governor of Massachusetts from 1800 until 1807, and again from 1812 until 1816. He was far more popular than his party. In his second term, he was the vocal leader of a divided New England against the War of 1812. He withheld the state militia from federal service when both the secretary of war and the president said it was essential to national survival.

By obeying the letter of the law, if not the spirit, he managed to finish his political life with his reputation intact.

Strong appeared tall and angular; a solid man. Though not brilliant, he had plain speech and sterling integrity. He had a judicious temperament and seemed always to be fair and thoughtful. His contemporaries noted his charm and engaging manner, which held him in good stead during difficult times. These personal qualities explain the gentle, even kindly, judgment of him at the end of his life.

He died, unexpectedly, of angina pectoris and was buried in the Bridge Street cemetery in Northampton, Massachusetts.

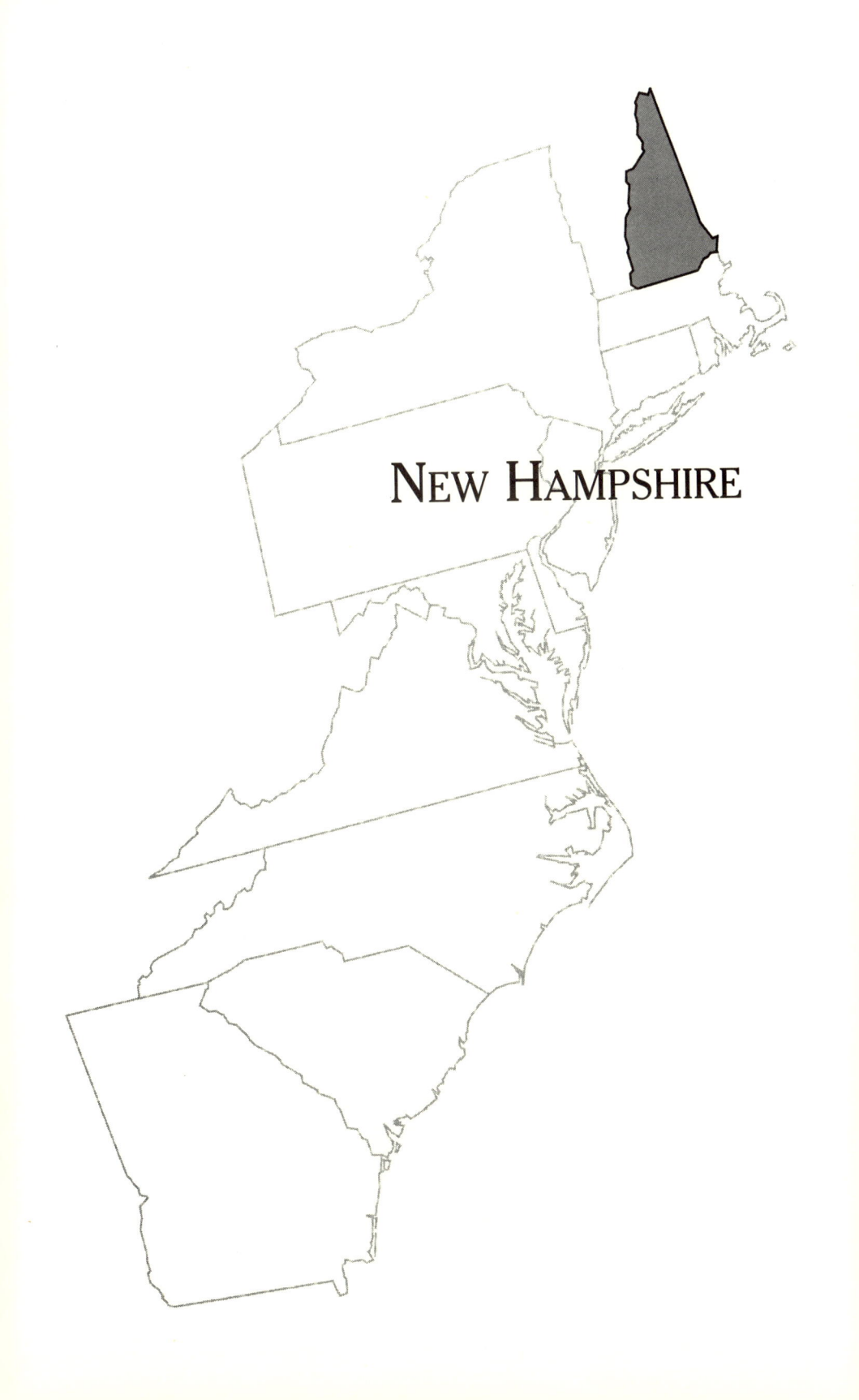

New Hampshire

JOHN LANGDON

June 26, 1741 *September 18, 1819*

    John Langdon was born in Portsmouth, New Hampshire. His father, a simple farmer, did not believe that any special education was necessary for his sons. Johns's mother, however, insisted upon only the best preparation. He was sent to the local Latin grammar school, and then was apprenticed in a counting house. At the close of his apprenticeship, he took to the sea, sailing in the West Indian trade, where he had many youthful escapades and love affairs. He was very ambitious, and disciplined himself to work and study hard. Within a fairly short time, he became a captain. Eventually, he bought several ships and by the outbreak of the Revolution he had acquired a comfortable fortune.

    In 1774, he was part of a group that seized the British munitions stored in Portsmouth. In 1775, when the royal governor fled, John Langdon led the fight for a new constitution. In 1776, he did double duty, first as speaker of the assembly in his state, and then in the Continental Congress, where he served on many committees.

When Langdon was the assembly speaker, he used his own money to stop a British incursion under Burgoyne. He was the leader of a militia group in the Battle of Saratoga in 1777, for which he received commendations and recognition. In that same year, Langdon married Elizabeth Sherburne who was from a wealthy family. She was sixteen years old and he was thirty-six. They had one daughter.

While in the Continental Congress, he campaigned for, and won, an appointment to the newly-created post of agent for marine affairs in New Hampshire. His compensation came from substantial commissions on all purchases made for the Congress and on the proceeds of all captured prize vessels and goods. Langdon liked power and money, and this appointment gave him both. He emerged from the revolution a very rich man. To avoid a conflict of interest, he was forced to give up his seat in the Congress.

Langdon, meanwhile, served in the Rhode Island campaign, was a delegate to the Congress in 1783, elected a state senator in 1784, elected governor in 1785, and again chosen to be speaker in the legislature for 1786-87.

He represented the state at the Constitutional Convention in Philadelphia and paid the expenses for the state's delegates. Unfortunately, they arrived when much of the work had been completed. Langdon supported a strong government, a strong national defense, and a program of taxation. He was especially interested in powers regulating commerce. Upon his return home, he became a member of the state ratifying convention.

Langdon was elected to the Senate, where he drew the six-year term, and was promptly chosen president *pro tempore* for the first and most of the second Congress. Thus, the duty to get the Senate organized, before John Adams was confirmed as vice-president, fell upon him. He was in charge of the electoral count for the first presidential election and consequently had the honor of officially informing Washington and Adams that they had been elected. He voted for Hamilton's financial plans and showed keen interest in the issues involving trade and tariffs. He supported the reduction of the tax on molasses because, as he said, it was the poor man's butter and the raw material for New England rum.

Surprisingly, he switched his politics and philosophy in a few years, and became a loyal supporter of more Jeffersonian principles. He argued vigorously against the Jay Treaty[5] with England. As early as 1789, a French minister noted his appreciation for, and sympathetic sentiments toward France, undoubtedly because of French help in the revolution. In 1798, he energetically opposed Adams's policies which were taking the nation into an undeclared war with France.

Langdon won a second term in 1795. When he retired from the Senate in 1801, Jefferson promptly offered him the position of secretary of the navy. He declined, so that he could build the Jeffersonian party in New Hampshire. Subsequently, he served in the state Legislature from 1801 to 1805. He contested for the governorship every year from 1805 until 1811. He won each time, except for 1809, which he lost because he supported Jefferson's embargo on exports to prevent war with England. Madison offered him the opportunity to run for vice-president in 1812, but he was sixty-one years old and he declined.

Langdon was handsome and had noble carriage. He was no genius, but had uncommon good sense. He had an inquiring and open mind, and good understanding of all issues. His motives were often questioned, and some suggested that he was too fond of money, but many testified to his generous, almost lavish, hospitality. His residence was elegant and well furnished. He was an interesting mix of opportunism, ambition and conviction. It was hard not to like him.

He died at age seventy-eight, and was interred in North Cemetery in Portsmouth.

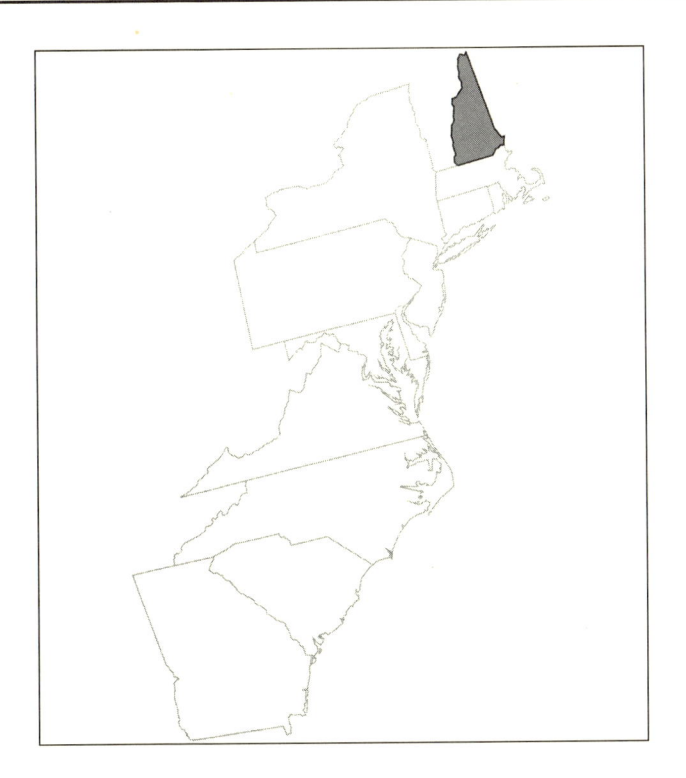

PAINE WINGATE

May 14, 1739   *March 7, 1838*

Paine Wingate's most lasting contributions came in his retirement, for he lived to the venerable age of ninety-nine, outliving all his contemporaries. As such a participant of our early history, he served as a firsthand source for historians. Giving his version of events, he was able to color the judgments of a host of writers.

A reluctant revolutionary, he took his first political position as a delegate to the state constitutional convention in 1781. In the early years of the revolutionary activity against England, Wingate frequently found himself in disagreement with the most radical elements working to break the ties binding us to the mother country. For example, he refused to sign the "Association Test" which proposed that every public figure sign the document to indicate support for the Declaration of Independence. Thus there was a widely held belief that he was in league with the local Tories, a sort of secret supporter of the monarchy and of our colonial ties to England. He was neither a supporter of the Tories nor a believer in a permanent colonial relationship. His religious scruples and innate approach to life just made him very conservative. Moreover, he always sought reconciliation when people differed sharply. He was not convinced that separation was necessary to achieve changes in the political life of the colonies.

Perhaps he learned some of his mediation skills from his position as the sixth of twelve children, of the Reverend Paine Wingate and his wife Mary. He studied theology at Harvard, graduating in 1759. Four years later, he was ordained pastor of the Congregational church at Hampton Falls. In 1765, he married Eunice Pickering of Salem, Massachusetts. Her brother, Timothy Pickering, exerted a strong influence on Paine's thinking. Pickering was very conservative, and had a gloomy pessimistic outlook. He was an influential member of the Essex Junto, from 1778 until 1812. This was a kind of club made up of lawyers and merchants who believed that they had to assume responsibility to look after their neighbor's conduct. Pickering convinced Wingate to support the Federalist's political positions. When the Essex Junto failed to support the War of 1812, they lost all influence.

The Wingates had two sons and three daughters. During these early years, his parish was theologically contentious, and the parishioners did not always see eye to eye with their minister. In 1771, Wingate offered to resign, effective in 1776. He then moved to a previously purchased farm in Stratham, where he lived for the rest of his long life. During the next few years, his absorbing interests were in improving his farm and in new farming techniques.

Finally, in 1781, Paine Wingate became active in the political life of his community. After service as a delegate to the state constitutional convention, he was elected to the state legislature. In 1787, he became a delegate to the last Congress under the Articles of Confederation. During the ratification debate in New Hampshire, he came forth as a very strong supporter of the Constitution, and that helped elect him to the first Senate of the United States.

He drew the four year term, which ended in 1793. He supported Federalist programs, but dissented on Hamilton's funding plans. He did not distinguish himself in the Senate, but he always paid careful attention to his committee work. He was not reelected to the Senate, but was sent, instead, to the House of Representatives. He failed reelection to the House because he was not considered reliable enough in his Federalist principles.

After his federal service, he was elected to one more term in the state legislature in 1795, and then was appointed judge of the state superior court. He held that post until 1809, when, at age seventy, he retired to his farm in Stratham. He was a very ordinary man without special talents, but one who was honorable in character and well intentioned.

Twenty-nine years later he died and was interred at Stratham Cemetery.

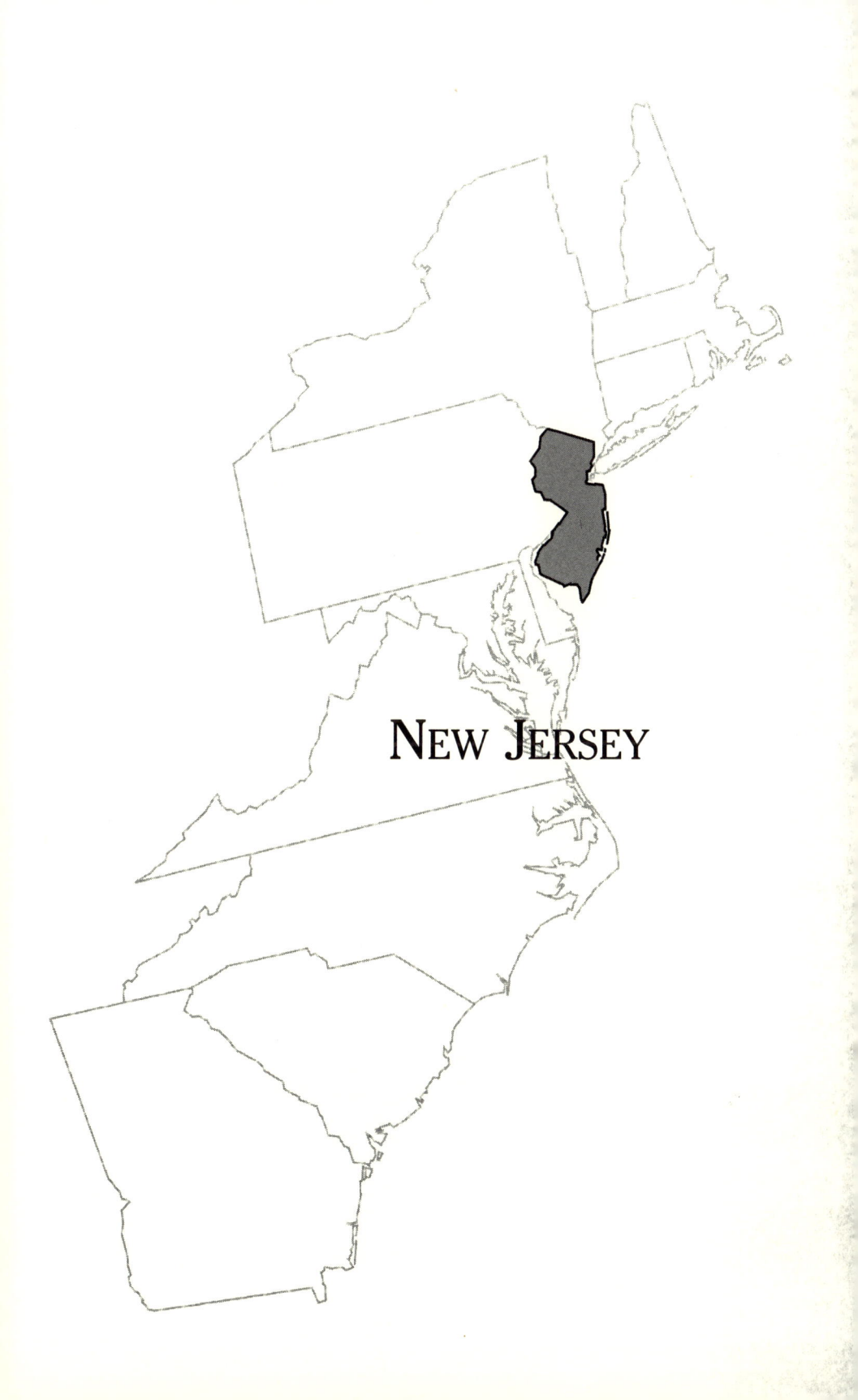

New Jersey

WILLIAM PATERSON
December 24, 1745   *September 9, 1806*

William Paterson's family voyaged from Ireland, landing in New Castle on the Delaware, in October 1745. Two months later William Paterson was born. After a few successful years of itinerant peddling the family settled in New Jersey where William's father began to manufacture tin plate, engage in general merchandising, and later sell real estate.

Not much of young William's early schooling is known. He graduated from the College of New Jersey[6] in 1766, having earned a master of arts degree. While at college he studied law in the office of Richard Stockton and was admitted to the bar in 1769. He moved several times while looking for a better area in which to develop his practice.

Paterson began his long and successful political career in 1775, as a deputy to the New Jersey Provincial Congress from Somerset County. In his second year, he was elected its assistant secretary and then secretary. In 1776, he became a member of the convention that wrote the state's revolutionary constitution.

For over a year he was an active member of the minute men and a member of the committee of safety. In 1776, Paterson was elected to the state's legislative council for a two year's term. In that same year he was chosen state attorney general, a job re-quiring travel to criminal courts in all the counties, which helped him develop a large following. In 1779, he married Cornelia Bell, a prosperous farmer's daughter. In 1780, he declined to serve in the Continental Congress because the job of traveling attorney general was so burdensome, and he eventually quit in 1783.

His wife gave birth to three children during the four years after they were married. She died after the birth of their third child. Two years later, Paterson married Euphemia White, whose father had acted as host for Paterson's first marriage.

A delegate to the Constitutional Convention in Philadelphia in 1787, Paterson objected to the power of the populous states. He introduced a plan for a unicameral legislature representing states, not individuals. States would have equal voting without regard to size, wealth, or population. He considered the struggle successful when the resulting compromise provided for a two-house legislature, one based on population, and the other based on state equality. Paterson was a signer of the Constitution and worked for adoption in his home state.

The New Jersey legislature chose him one of the state's first senators. Paterson drew a four-year term, but only served for eighteen months. He was appointed to the committee to count the electoral votes for president and vice-president, the first task to be completed by the Senate. He wrote the first nine sections of the act which established the judicial system. In general, he supported a strong presidency, voting for the president's power to remove officers once appointed, and for all of Hamilton's plans which came up for a vote, before he resigned his seat.

Senator Maclay of Pennsylvania labeled him a Hamilton helper, suggesting that he was willing to speak about any topic to delay proceedings, even if he had nothing to say about the subject, and that Paterson was more concerned with personal interest than he was in the national welfare. William Pierce, a colleague from the Constitutional Convention, however, wrote that Paterson's powers created wonder and astonishment. He saw him as a man of great modesty, a scholar, a lawyer, and an orator who was praised by everyone.

When Paterson was elected to succeed Governor William

Livingston, who died in office, he resigned his Senate seat. By authorization of the legislature, Paterson collected and codified all the English statutes, that were still on the books, governing the state's residents. It was a monumental task that took him from 1792 until 1800. In addition, he developed *Paterson's Practice Laws*, which modernized the rules of practice and procedure in the state's common law and chancery courts. When a new industrial town was chartered on the Passaic River in 1790, it seemed appropriate to name it for him.

Washington appointed Paterson an associate justice of the Supreme Court in 1793, and he held the position until 1806. At age sixty-one, with his health failing, he headed toward Ballston Springs, a New York spa. He died while in his daughter's Albany home, and she arranged for his burial in the vault of the Van Rensselaer Manor House near Albany.

PHILEMON DICKINSON
April 5, 1739 *February 4, 1809*

   Philemon Dickinson lost the Senate race against William Paterson in 1789, but upon Paterson's resignation, was elected to fill his unexpired term. His father was Samuel Dickinson, Chief Justice of Delaware, and his brother John Dickinson was the author of the widely read *Letters of a Pennsylvania Farmer*. He was born in Talbot County, Maryland, or near Dover, Delaware. William Killen, a law student in his father's office and later Chancellor of Delaware, was his first tutor.

   In 1755, he entered the College of Philadelphia and graduated four years later. The college has an interesting history. It began as the Charity School of Philadelphia in 1740, was converted into the Academy of Philadelphia in 1751 with Ben Franklin as first President of the trustees, changed its name again and chartered as the College and Academy of Philadelphia in 1755. Then the legislature of Pennsylvania changed the name to the University of the

State of Pennsylvania in 1779, finally shortening it to the University of Pennsylvania in 1791. It was the first institution in America to be styled a university.

As his father's health began to fail, in 1761, he gradually took over the management of the huge family estates, while continuing to study law in his brother's office in Philadelphia. At this time, he married his cousin, Mary Cadwalader. When she died, he married her sister, Rebecca.

The Dickinson brothers became active in political affairs after 1765. Philemon was appointed colonel of the New Jersey militia in 1775. Without interrupting his military activities, he served for one year, 1776, in the provincial congress of New Jersey. In the following year with four hundred untrained militia he decisively defeated an expedition sent to New Jersey by General Cornwallis. Governor Livingston then appointed him major-general and commander-in-chief of the militia. He was given credit for the victory when he invaded Staten Island. In 1778, he delayed General Clinton's progress through New Jersey by destroying all bridges. This helped to bring about the victory at the Battle of Monmouth.

Dickinson challenged Governor Livingston for New Jersey's highest office three times, losing in every attempt. Since he was a large property owner in Delaware, and thus eligible to hold office, he was elected to the Confederation Congress from Delaware in 1782. His only contribution to the work of the Congress was on the committee to recommend a site for a new capital. From 1785 to 1792, he managed the family farms, finally reentering public life when he was appointed to fill Paterson's unexpired Senate term. Senator Maclay had very little to say about Dickinson, but the few references are all favorable. They shared negative views about Hamilton, and they talked often about senatorial affairs. Unlike his brother, Dickinson was not original in his thinking, nor was he an able debater who could succeed in influencing events. He was a very decent and honorable man, of ordinary talents, who left no lasting impress on the nation's legal or intellectual history. The short time he had in the Senate ended on March 3, 1793. He spent his retirement years at his country home, The Hermitage, near Trenton.

Interment was in the Friends Meeting House Burying Ground in Trenton.

JONATHAN ELMER

November 29, 1745 *September 3, 1817*

Jonathan Elmer, the only doctor to serve in the first Senate was born in New Jersey. His frail constitution and sickly health caused his parents concern, and they decided he had to have a good education. After rigorous private tutoring he enrolled in medical school at the University of Pennsylvania. While still a student in 1769, he married Mary Seeley. Between 1766 and 1771 he earned two degrees and then began medical practice. In the same year that he hung out his shingle, he also became sheriff of Cumberland County and a member of the local vigilance committee. He and his wife were both members of the Presbyterian church and remained so for the rest of their lives. In later years he became a ruling elder and eventually a delegate to the general assembly.

As a result of his research and writing on the eye and on airborne diseases Elmer gained membership in the American

Philosophical Society in 1772. However, he preferred political and legal business more than medicine and became active in those fields.

While serving for three years in the provincial congress he remained active in military affairs. In that congress he was elected head of the Bridgeton Association which published *The Plain Dealer*, a patriotic news letter. He was appointed captain, later major, of a light-infantry company, while holding the position of county clerk from 1776 to 1789. He was elected to the Continental Congress in 1776, and was assigned to the army medical committee which inspected and approved hospitals in New Jersey and Pennsylvania. Although his appointment to Congress was renewed he felt the salary was insufficient and returned to his private practice in 1778. He served for many years on the New Jersey executive council as well as in the Confederation Congress, where he worked effectively to support a federal Constitution.

He was elected to the first Senate, where he drew a two-year term. He was a consistent champion of Washington and Hamilton. He ran into political trouble because his constituents wanted the national capital to be in Philadelphia, but he voted for the Potomac River site. As a result, he failed to be reelected in 1791. He never lost his interest in politics and government, but practiced medicine for the next twenty years before running for office as surrogate judge. He won that office in 1813, but a year later made the decision to retire.

Elmer was a first-rate student and scholar. He was thorough and diligent in mastering issues and he had flexibility to change, when necessary, in all matters short of those involving principle. Colleagues thought him formal in his manners and stately in bearing. No one ever mentioned that he had a sense of humor. He ended his life with a considerable fortune, and there is evidence that he paid attention to securing financial security before all else.

He died in Burlington, New Jersey and was buried in the old Presbyterian cemetery.

New York

RUFUS KING

March 24, 1755   *April 29, 1827*

    Rufus King, the only man in the first Senate who was considered by many to have the character and leadership to be a future president, was in public life for forty-six years with no hint of scandal. The testimony to his ability and character is overwhelming. Hamilton saw him as well informed and very judicious. Jeremiah Mason, a friend from Senate days, said King was the most able man and greatest orator he had ever met. Daniel Webster described him as a speaker of strength, dignity, fire and unequaled ease. One friend said that he was a gentleman with a handsome face, strong expressive eyes and a sweet high-toned voice. Finally one fellow senator said he could be rude when he chose and that he had a talent for exposing the weakness in an opponent's argument, but was charming and talented. Who was this man held in such high regard by his colleagues?

King was born in Maine. He was given an excellent education, first at the Dummer Academy in Byfield and then at Harvard University. Although his father was an unbending Tory, Rufus King became a committed revolutionary. After graduation he apprenticed for law with Theophilus Parsons. He opened his own practice in 1780, in Newburyport, Massachusetts. His sharp and compelling legal wisdom, his already polished oratorical skills and his considerable charm won wide admiration and he was sent to the state general court in 1782-83. During this time he participated in General Sullivan's unsuccessful expedition against Rhode Island. When he was twenty-eight years old, Massachusetts sent him to the Confederation Congress from 1784 to 1787. King tried to get all states to pay their share of the costs of the Congress. He also attempted to prevent the spread of slavery into the Northwest Territory. He would remain against slavery throughout his public life. In this four-year period he displayed his enormous talents and played a major role.

On March 30, 1786 King married Mary Alsop, whose wealthy father was a politically well-connected New York merchant. Over the next ten years the couple would have five sons.

The following year King was one of five Massachusetts delegates sent to the Constitutional Convention. He was the only New Englander to arrive on the opening day May 21, 1787. He was adept at correcting faulty motions, clarifying confused points and conciliating. He defended a strong executive and a strong central government which he thought were necessary to keep law and order. He believed in the separation of powers, argued for representation based solely on population, and thought the sanctity of contracts was beyond argument. In keeping with his principles, he advocated placing a tax on slaves as a way to limit slavery, and wanted a time limit placed on the importation of slaves. Finally, he was on the committee on style that gave final shape to the document.

By this time King was thirty-two, had been married for two years and was growing close to the Alsops who were urging him to move to New York. Hamilton and Washington, with whom he had a growing friendship, also encouraged him to consider a move. King was given much credit for his leadership in the struggle for Constitutional adoption in Massachusetts. Shortly after the ratification he made he his move to New York. Within a month, he was elected to the state assembly.

In short order Washington and Hamilton backed him as candidate for the Senate from New York. Four months after the opening on July 17, 1789, he became its youngest member at thirty-four. He held this distinction until James Monroe was elected and took the Virginia seat on December 6, 1790. Monroe was thirty-two years old. King drew the six-year term. He was active on thirty-six committees, including those on fixing compensation for the president and vice-president, statehood for Vermont, authorizing and arranging the first census, and the funding bill. King helped arrange the compromise on the location of the new capital and for the assumption of state debts. He supported all Hamilton's financial plans with vigor and conviction, and was appointed a director of the national bank in 1791. He worked to get approval for John Jay's mission to England and to get the Jay Treaty[7] passed.

He made the charge and spearheaded the fight against the right of Albert Gallatin to take a Senate seat on the grounds that he had not been a citizen for the required nine years. Gallatin, who was a supporter of Jefferson's principals and represented the agricultural interests of western Pennsylvania, was elected to the Senate by the Pennsylvania Federalist legislature on a joint ballot 45 - 37 in February 1793. By any fair interpretation of the Constitution, Gallatin was entitled to his Senate seat but the Federalist Senate, for political reasons, voted 14 - 12 to deny it.

According to Senator Maclay, King spoke often and was very regular in attendance. Maclay also noted that his character was detestable and that he lacked candor. No doubt he was reacting to King's total support for Hamilton as well as because King had accepted appointment as a national bank director.

Though reelected in 1795, King soon resigned to accept Washington's appointment as minister to Britain. He was an effective ambassador, serving through the Adams administration, and for two years under Jefferson. Relieved at his own request in 1802, he returned to Jamaica, New York, to begin life as a farmer.

After the British burned the Capitol he raised money for the rebuilding. The Federalists pressed him to run as vice-presidential candidate in 1804 and again in 1808. He lost. He opposed entering the war of 1812 but, once the country was at war, he patriotically supported it. The Federalists even persuaded him to be their presidential candidate in 1816. In that year of Good Feelings, Monroe won all but one of the electoral votes, making King the last Federalist to run for that office. Following this defeat King was elected to the House of Representatives. There he opposed rechartering the national bank, authored the Navigation Act which fixed United States policy on the sea, and worked successfully to improve trade. In 1819 he was returned to the Senate. In the debates over admitting Missouri into the Union, King took the lead in opposing the extension of slavery. He opposed any compromise, including that proposed by Henry Clay. He also wrote a measure, which passed in 1820, lowering the price of public lands and mandating cash payment. The following year King was on the committee to write a new constitution for New York State. His argument against a "white only" voting clause prevailed but, as finally written, the constitution limited the black vote to males owning a $250 freehold. Although he refused renomination to the Senate in 1825, in order to retire, President John Quincy Adams appointed him minister to Great Britain once more. Reluctantly, he agreed to accept. Within a month of his arrival, he grew ill and had to resign, returning home in June 1826.

He spent the rest of his life promoting reform and advancing the cause of education, especially at Columbia College. He remained active in affairs of the Episcopal church, until he died at age seventy-two, and was buried with honors in the cemetery of Grace Church in Jamaica, New York.

PHILIP SCHUYLER
November 11, 1733 *November 18, 1804*

Philip Schuyler was born in Albany, New York. He attended common schools, finishing his education under a private tutor in New Rochelle, New York. He was fourth generation Dutch, with deep roots in the patroon culture that prevailed throughout his lifetime. His father died when Philip was eight years old, leaving him the sole heir of his vast estates. In September 1755, at age twenty-two, he married Catherine Van Rensselaer, an intelligent woman of strong character. They shared forty-eight years of political and social life.

When the French and Indian War started in 1754, Schuyler became captain of a company he recruited, and was battle-tested at Lake George. That winter he became the commissary for a large army force under an English officer. Since his lands produced everything that troops needed, he was able to provision the army and turn a handsome profit. In 1760 he had to go to England to square the accounts and in 1764 he was honored with membership in the Society of Arts in London.

During these years, he also added to his large landholdings, entered the Hudson River trade and recruited immigrants from Europe. Within a few years, he added sawmills, gristmills and the first flaxmill in the colonies. He began extensive lumbering operations as well. As he grew in wealth and power, he resented any interference by parliament, or by royal colonial officers, in his operations. His fight paralleled that of the Sons of Liberty, but he never felt any affinity for their cause, nor did he condone violence.

He declined to serve in the first Continental Congress due to ill health but accepted a seat in the second Continental Congress. He served on a committee to prepare rules for the Continental Army. Once Washington was appointed commander-in-chief he appointed Schuyler one of four major-generals. Washington put him in charge of New York in order to pacify the Indians before attempting an invasion of Canada.

His military career was less than successful. During the Burgoyne campaign of 1777 he was reprimanded by Congress for lack of command ability. Schuyler blamed a weak army, poor discipline, insufficient financial support, the hostility of New Englanders and the enmity of other generals. His opponents charged him with incompetence, with being an extreme disciplinarian who caused problems with the troops, with being afraid to tangle with the British, and with disloyalty. A court martial exonerated him. In spring, 1779 his resignation from the army was accepted. He remained on the Board of Commissioners for Indian Affairs reporting to Congress about the Indian menace on the frontier. In spite of all these difficulties he maintained a strong presence in the early government.

Schuyler reported to Congress on the depreciated currency in 1779 and 1780, and made recommendations for issuing new bills of credit. His recommendations were adopted. He also served as headquarters committee chairman assisting Washington with staff changes, and in developing ways to cooperate with the French.

He served in the state Senate from 1780 to 1784 and again from 1786 to 1789. During this period he advocated more power for state and national government while continuing his support for funding the state debt. He believed that states should surrender claims to western lands and that Congress should control interstate and foreign commerce. Alexander Hamilton, who married Schuyler's daughter Elizabeth, had the political skills to make that philosophy a reality.

Schuyler's election to the Senate of the United States in 1789 was no surprise. He drew the two-year term and was not reelected in 1791. Though appointed to twenty-four committees, he only worked on ten of them. He was concerned with finances, Indian affairs, war pensions, and supporting the military establishment.

Schuyler supported every increase in presidential power, every excise tax, funding the state debts and every pro-military measure. Schuyler was called the chief cheerleader for the Military Establishment Bill, by Senator Maclay, who saw it as the foundation of an undesirable, standing army.

When Schuyler returned to New York he was elected to the state Senate, serving from 1792 until 1797, at which time he was again elected to the federal Senate. Poor health forced a resignation before a year was out.

Schuyler was a strong, well-developed, commanding presence. He dressed fashionably and with great care. Many found him arrogant, and complained about his austere manner. His home life and large family, three sons and five daughters, was apparently a happy one. Bayard Tuckerman, Schuyler's 1904 fawning biographer, wrote what could be an appropriate epitaph.

"His career, honorable to himself, useful to the community in which his lot was cast and to the nation which he helped to found, owed its success to sterling qualities of head and heart. Without genius, without extraordinary talent in any particular, he had that combination of ability and character which makes a trusted leader."

He died at his Albany mansion and was placed in the Van Rensselaer-Schuyler family vault. Years later, the remains were removed to the Albany Rural cemetery, and buried with military honors.

North Carolina

BENJAMIN HAWKINS

August 15, 1754 *June 6, 1818*

Benjamin Hawkins, at thirty-five, was the second youngest man elected to the first Senate. He grew up in a family committed to the revolution and to independence. His father, a member of the state general assembly for thirteen years, had raised the first revolutionary volunteer company in his region, served as a colonel in the Revolution and became a member of the state convention that ratified the Constitution.

Young Hawkins attended the College of New Jersey,[8] where he majored in the classics and languages, becoming proficient in French. The college was closed during his senior year because of the revolutionary war. For over a year, Hawkins filled the need for reliable French translators on Washington's staff. He was at the Battle of Monmouth and other New Jersey engagements, and then became purchasing agent for arms and ammunition. During this time he married Livinia Downs. They had one son and four daughters and were a close-knit family.

From 1781 to 1784, and again from 1786 to 1787, he was in the Confederation Congress. In his second term he served on a committee assigned to negotiate with Indian tribes in the southern states. The committee had to write treaties defining the tribal boundaries of the Cherokees, Choctaws and Chickasaws. This experience cemented a lifelong commitment to building better relationships between the Indians and white. North Carolina did not ratify the Constitution until November 1789, and Hawkins, elected to the first Senate, was not sworn in until January 13, 1790, when the Senate had finished the first year of its first session. He drew the six-year term and entered the Senate with a reputation as a strong Federalist. He was a quiet supporter of Hamilton's program, dissenting only on some tariff rates which would have affected his constituency. One colleague described him, at this time, as an aristocrat, proud, wealthy and very conservative. Senator Maclay noted that Hawkins was neither self-assured nor a forceful speaker. Maclay commended his vote "on the ethical side" of the southern soldiers arrears pay bill, voting to pay them the money that they had coming. When his term expired on March 3, 1795, Hawkins was defeated in his bid for reelection. All was not lost, though. Washington immediately appointed him as federal negotiator with the Creek Confederacy. Through his sincere and ardent efforts Hawkins got Creek approval for a treaty in 1796, which kept the peace for some years. This achievement led to his double appointment, as federal agent to the Creeks, and as general superintendent of Indian tribes south of the Ohio River. His family tried to dissuade him from accepting the appointment, for he had never had a chance to use his education in the classics. Furthermore, he had inherited great wealth, large landholdings and many slaves, and his wife and children felt that these family possessions needed tending. By this time in his life he had earned the respect of his neighbors and was much honored by them. He resisted the family arguments, gave up the comfortable life, and devoted himself to the welfare of the Indians and to protecting their rights. He took his responsibility very seriously and met it so effectively that the four presidents after Washington refused to accept his resignation and renewed his appointment at every expiration date.

He was given the title, "Beloved Man of the Four Nations," by the Indians. Using his slaves, he built a model farm, and trained Indians in grain production and cattle farming. Skilled slave craftsmen taught Indians coopering, tool making, house building and all the skills used on successful southern plantations. He is credited with keeping the peace in the region.

During the War of 1812 the British fomented unrest among the

Indians and encouraged them to attack frontier settlements. Hawkins organized a friendly Creek regiment led by a half-Indian, William McIntosh, and reluctantly joined Andrew Jackson in crushing the uprising. As punishment, the Indian Confederacy was forced to cede huge amounts of land, including large tracts that belonged to the Creeks who fought on the side of the United States. Hawkins was terribly disappointed that his life's work came to such a sorry end.

He wrote extensively about Indian life. Especially significant is his *Sketch of the Creek Country.* He was noted for beginning to change white attitudes toward the Indian.

His contributions to the success of the new nation, and in fact to humanity, gained some recognition and many honors. Hawkinsville, Georgia, is named for him and he was one of the first trustees of the University of North Carolina.

A good Indian affairs administrator, he continued in that post until his death, in 1818 at age sixty-two. Family members blamed the war and the breakdown in Indian/white relations for hurrying his death. He was buried on a plantation overlooking the Flint River near the site of his Indian headquarters called the Old Agency.

SAMUEL JOHNSTON

December 15, 1733　　　　　　　　　　*August 17, 1816*

Samuel Johnston was born in Dundee, Scotland. He was three years old when his parents brought him to North Carolina. His uncle, Gabriel Johnston, was the colonial governor from 1730 to 1752. With help from relatives, Samuel's father acquired large land holdings in a short time, making life quite comfortable for the family. He received his early schooling in New Haven, Connecticut. In 1754 Johnston returned to Edenton, North Carolina where he began the study of law. He became a member of the colonial assembly and held other public positions as early as 1759. He would continue in these until 1775. Among the positions he held for many years was clerk of the court for the Edenton district and, at various times, the deputy officer for maritime matters for the port of Edenton. After he finished his education he married Frances Cathcart of Edenton. They had one son. In 1765 they moved to Hayes, his beautiful home on Albemarle Sound.

In addition to his active political life he began to practice law in 1767.

Justice and the law became central to his views. When the Carolina frontiersmen revolted in the Regulator War against unfair taxes, Johnston thought their actions were illegal. He drafted the "Bloody Act" to forcibly suppress them. On the other hand, recognizing the legitimacy of their claims, he led the assembly to pass many reforms. Similarly, he always viewed the struggle with England from a judicial perspective. He opposed the Stamp Act because he thought it was illegal. Early in the struggle for independence he became the recognized leader of the movement in North Carolina.

In 1773 he became a member of the Committee of Correspondence. He was a delegate to the first four colonial congresses. That body elected him their president in the last two terms.

By 1775 he was on the Council of Safety, one of the treasurers for the colony, as well as paymaster for district troops. The council made him a member of the committee to codify all the laws. North Carolina was the first state to declare independence from England.

In that year, between the time the royal governor abdicated and the first governor under the state's revolutionary constitution took office, Johnston was the executive authority. He worked to restore law and order, as well as to preserve the rights and privileges of traditional English liberty. He was a powerful presence at the state convention and was given credit for developing the state constitution.

While he accepted the principle of popular government, he opposed universal manhood suffrage. He believed annual elections would protect minority rights, but he urged lifetime appointments for judges.

For three years after 1779 he was sent to the state Senate and for two years, 1781-82, he was a member of the Confederation Congress. In 1781 he declined its presidency and announced his intention to retire the following year. In 1785 he joined the committee settling the dispute over the Massachusetts-New York border.

Johnston was elected governor three times in a row in 1787-88-89. As governor he was the presiding officer of the two conventions called to consider ratification of the federal Constitution. The first convention rejected ratification, but the second approved. Thus, he was thoroughly familiar with the document and his support of it was unconditional. He resigned the governorship when he was elected to the Senate.

He took his seat on November 27, 1789, drawing the four-year term. Since North Carolina was late in ratifying the Constitution, Johnston, like Hawkins, missed the first year and almost a month of the second session of the Senate.

There are only a few recorded references concerning Johnston's work in the Senate. He was a Federalist who differed with Hamilton only on the question of how to fund the debt. Johnston exuded confidence in himself and in his opinions, and he was well prepared in the law. In spite of his three years as governor the people of North Carolina did not show love or affection for Johnston. His most powerful asset was his family's wealth and standing, which helps explain why he reached high office. He was a rather minor figure in the Senate and had a very poor attendance record. This did not go unnoticed. Before the time for his reelection the state legislature asked him to give an accounting of his record in the federal Senate. Johnston refused, losing reelection as a result.

Johnston's career is not without merit. He had made his greatest contributions to the nation during and immediately after the Revolution. He was the first trustee of the University of North Carolina, serving for twelve years. His last official position was as a Superior Court Judge from 1800 until 1803, when he retired at seventy years of age. He spent the rest of his life with his family at Hayes. He died near his home, and was interred in the Johnston family burial ground on the Hayes plantation near Edenton.

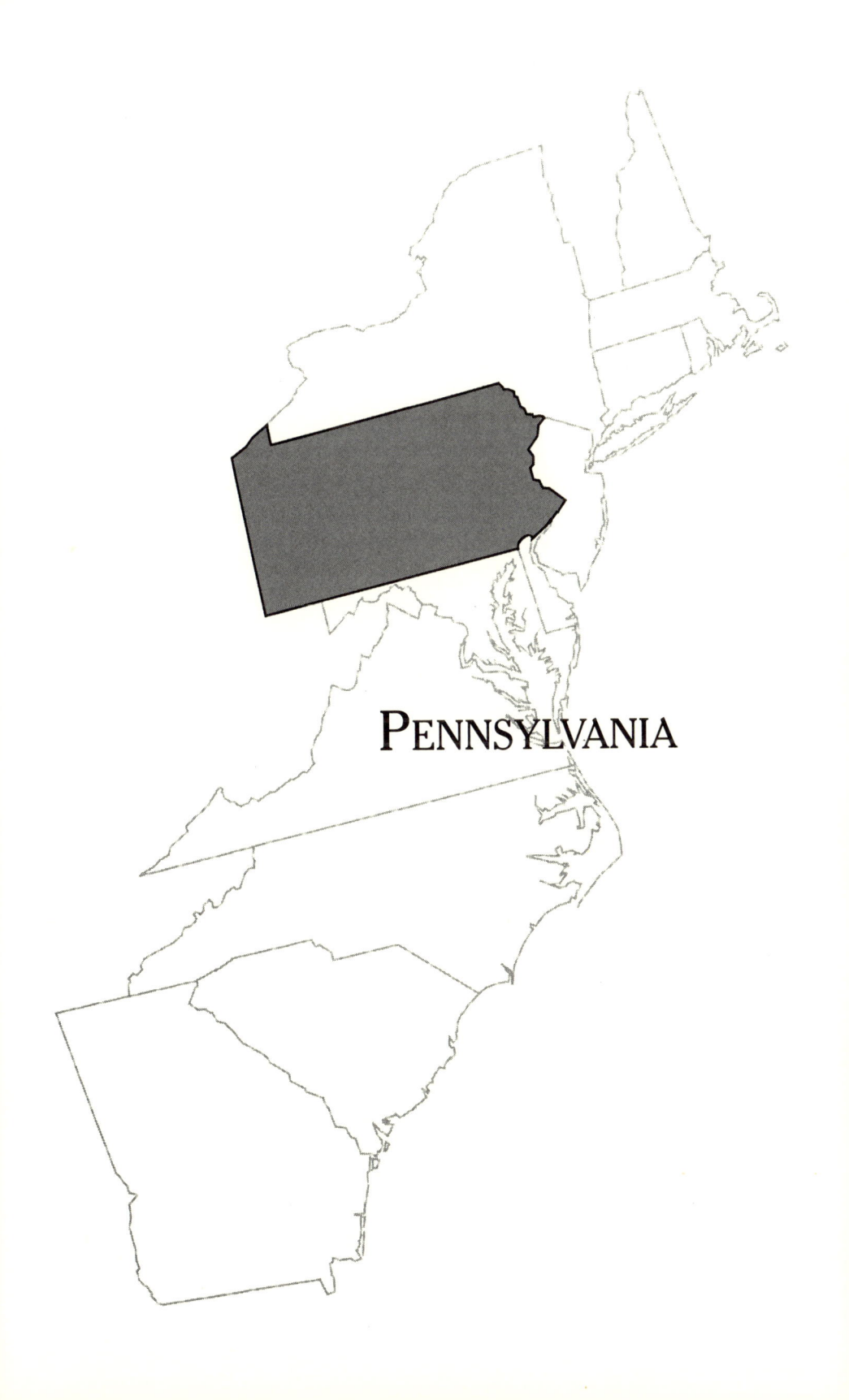

PENNSYLVANIA

WILLIAM MACLAY

July 27, 1734　　　　　　　　　　　　　　*April 16, 1804*

　　William Maclay, whose Scotch-Irish father settled in America in 1734, was born in Garden City, Pennsylvania. He received a classical education in a local school run by the Reverend John Blair.

　　As a young man he became a lieutenant in the French and Indian War, where he saw action at Fort Duquesne, and in other Indian battles. When the war ended in 1763 he met with the colonial proprietors in England about the development of central and western Pennsylvania. Thomas Penn was impressed with his ideas. He put him in charge of surveying. While serving in this capacity he laid out the town of Sunbury, bought considerable land and developed a large farm in Mifflintown. He held other offices simultaneously. He studied law, and was admitted to the bar in 1760. In 1769 he married Mary McClure, whose father founded Harrisburg.

From the beginning of the struggle for independence Maclay made a commitment to the revolutionary cause. During the war he was a member of the local militia, organized the frontier defense and was in charge of issuing commissary supplies in the Sunbury region. At the end of the war he was elected to the assembly, served on the state executive council, was judge of the court of common pleas, was deputy surveyor and was one of the commissioners who had to enforce laws governing Susquehanna River navigation. His most important job was negotiating with Indians to purchase lands.

Maclay, the first elected federal senator from his state, drew the short term. Of the men who served in the first Senate only William Maclay left a full record of all his thoughts. He was a forceful and outspoken opponent of loose construction of the Constitution, of the funding of the state debt, the tariff, the national bank, and the excise tax. In all matters related to monarchical ceremonies, titles and manners in public life he led the fight for more democratic forms and for equality of treatment of citizen and official alike. He was committed to establishing more democratic values and understood the importance of words and symbols in shaping them. He was a warmhearted man devoted to the public interest, especially to small, independent farmers. He was appalled by widespread greed among his colleagues as they voted their self-interest. He was vehemently opposed to speculation in public debt certificates by members of the Senate. His was a democratic voice, and an honest one, in the first Senate, which sorely needed both. Only Richard Henry Lee challenged the Senate leadership and the executive branch as regularly.

Maclay took great political risks fighting against the Hamiltonian program. He objected to Washington's presence in the Senate when business was being conducted because he was sure that the president's presence would inhibit the independence of some senators. He also considered that it was a violation of separation of powers. Moreover, he said so with Washington in the room and did it when no one else dared because of the aura surrounding the father of his country. His forthrightness reminded everyone that no man was above the law.

He was not reelected in 1791. Upon his return home he built a stone mansion on his farm near Harrisburg. In the following years his neighbors sent him to the state House of Representatives, (1795 and 1803), made him a presidential elector (1796), and an associate judge of the county (1801-03).

The last entry in his diary is the most moving and makes clear what a price he paid for standing by his convictions. As his time in the Senate ended he wrote,

"I stayed a moment to pack up my papers. Dalton alone came to me, and said he supposed we two would not see each other soon. ...As I left the Hall, I gave it a look with that kind of satisfaction which a man feels on leaving a place where he has been ill at ease, being fully satisfied that many a culprit has served two years at the wheelbarrow without feeling half the pain and mortification that I experienced in my honorable station."

He died in Harrisburg, at age seventy, and was buried in Paxton churchyard.

ROBERT MORRIS

January 31, 1734   *May 8, 1806*

    Shortly after Robert Morris was born in Liverpool, England in 1734 his father sailed to America. Robert, who would later be called the financier of the American Revolution, joined his father when he was thirteen. After a short time with a tutor Robert was apprenticed to Charles Willing, a major Philadelphia merchant. Morris was capable, reliable and ambitious. At the age of twenty he formed a partnership with his employer's son, Thomas Willing. It lasted for thirty-nine years, becoming the largest commercial trading company in the colonies.

    He was involved in many aspects of political life. He signed the non-importation agreement in 1765, opposed the hated Stamp Act and actively supported all American rights against Great Britain. Colonial Governor John Penn appointed him to the Board of Wardens for the port of Philadelphia.

He was six feet tall and a commanding presence. He was very successful and very active in the movement for independence by the time he married Mary White, the daughter of a successful farmer, in 1769. They would have five boys and two girls.

He was elected to the colonial assembly in 1775, was assigned to the committee of public safety and later became its vice-president. In that year he was sent to the Second Continental Congress where he was chairman of a secret committee to procure arms and ammunition. He also served on the ways and means and the naval affairs committees. In late 1775 the secret committee signed a contract with Willing and Morris to purchase arms and ammunition abroad. Initially he spoke against adopting the Declaration of Independence as premature, but eventually he signed the document, one of the four senators who did so. He was one of only two men to have had the triple distinction of signing both the Declaration of Independence and the United States Constitution as well as serving as a member of the first Senate.

When the Congress moved to Baltimore he remained behind to attend to what he called pressing financial business. This was a most unusual thing to do for one engaged so deeply in the public's financial business and many questions were raised about his conduct. There is no doubt that he used his financial know-how and his many business connections to contribute to the success of the revolution yet there were always questions about the accuracy of his reports and about some of his connections and transactions. He continued as financial manager through 1778, when he was made chair of the committee on finance. His committee drew up contracts and committed large sums of money and he regularly took his profits, broker fees and commissions.

In December 1778 he was elected to the state assembly but continued to make purchases for the army, sometimes on his own credit. In 1780 Morris organized the Bank of Pennsylvania and in 1782 he founded the Bank of North America which lent the United States $400,000. Within months of making the loan Congress appointed Morris the superintendent of finance. During his tenure as superintendent a contemporary said Morris was active, zealous, bold, enterprising and popular. John Adams said that Morris was masterly, open and honest but that he pursued gainful ends. Thomas Paine dissented, accusing Morris of engaging in private commercial activities while in public office. A congressional committee examined his books and exonerated him.

Morris was a delegate to the Annapolis Convention in 1786 and to the Constitutional Convention in 1787. He played a very minor role in the proceedings. After ratification Washington offered him the position of Secretary of the Treasury but Morris declined, suggesting Hamilton for the job. He preferred election to the first Senate and he used his friends and his financial influence to win the office. He drew the long term serving until March 3, 1795, when he returned full-time to his business activities. He was in total agreement with Hamilton's financial program, much of which he had been advocating for years.

He appears to have been a wheeler-dealer type. His colleague, Senator Maclay, found him secretive, unreliable and uncooperative. Morris was adamantly in favor of the Falls of the Delaware River as the site for the national capital. Eventually Maclay learned that Morris had swapped farms in Western Pennsylvania for land at the Delaware site. Morris was also speculating in debt certificates and in western lands and he sold thousands of acres to Europeans before he even owned those parcels. Maclay objected to these practices. They differed over most issues but were especially vitriolic over the issue of senatorial pay.

After Morris left the Senate he was the first to send a ship to Canton, China and extended his trade through China and the East Indies. In addition he organized the North American Land Company to purchase land in western New York and the Old Northwest. He overextended himself in this speculative venture and lost everything. Deeply in debt, he was sent to prison for over three months.

Morris had a penetrating and logical mind. Among his many achievements were the introduction of the icehouse and the successful use of the hothouse. Morrisville, Pennsylvania, was named for him.

He died in Philadelphia at age seventy-two and was buried there in the William White vault, in the yard of Christ Church.

RHODE ISLAND

THEODORE FOSTER

May 10, 1752　　　　　　　　　　　　　　*January 13, 1828*

When Theodore was born in Brookfield, Massachusetts, his father was a judge of the State Superior Court. Young Foster received a classical education. In 1770 he was a member of the second class to graduate from the College of Rhode Island, located in the town of Warren. The college was founded in 1764, moved to Providence in 1770, closed during the Revolution from 1776 to 1783 and started functioning in 1784. In 1804 the name was changed to Brown University to honor the son of the founder, Nicholas Brown, whose generous monetary gift made it possible to upgrade the facilities.

Foster also received a Master of Arts degree from Dartmouth College in 1786. He studied law and began his practice in Providence. Shortly after graduation he married Lydia Fenner. Her father was elected governor a few years later. Theodore and Lydia had three children.

In 1776 Foster was elected to the general assembly and held that position until 1782, earning the respect of his constituents and colleagues. He also served in the lower branch in later years. At a subsequent time the assembly authorized the formation of the town of Foster in his honor. After state service he was appointed Town Clerk of Providence. From 1775 to 1785 he collaborated with former governor Stephen Hopkins in collecting colonial artifacts. Their foresight eventually provided the basis for the Rhode Island Historical Society collection.

In 1785 he was appointed judge of the State Admiralty Court. When Rhode Island tried to solve her economic problems during the critical period by issuing paper money, in 1788 he spoke out against the practice and gained statewide recognition. He favored the adoption of the new federal Constitution when it was unpopular in the state. Over a year after the new government had been organized, Rhode Island finally ratified the Constitution.

Foster was elected to the federal Senate in May 1790 and took his seat on June 25. The state legislature had to lend Foster and fellow senator Joseph Stanton the money to pay for the trip. Fifteen months of the twenty-three month session had passed by the time the Rhode Island senators took their seats in the Senate. Foster drew the two-year term, was reelected in 1791 and again in 1797.

He chose not to run in 1802 thus his time in the Senate came to an end on March 3, 1803. It is interesting to note that his brother, Dwight, joined him in the Senate, the first brothers to serve concurrently. They also retired simultaneously, in 1803.

Foster supported the entire Hamiltonian program, including the Jay treaty[9]. He played a most unimportant role in the Senate where, other than his votes, his presence made no real difference to anyone. He did not like Jefferson, actively supporting Adams and then Aaron Burr. He accompanied Washington on his first official visit to Rhode Island in August 1790, which may well have been the highlight of his public life. By his own account he spent much time in the book stores of Philadelphia, the capital, for the second session of the first Congress (1790), browsing through shops looking for antiques and artifacts for his historical collection. He rarely missed a public lecture and frequently attended the theater.

In 1794 he was appointed a trustee of Brown University, holding that post until 1822. While in Philadelphia he lived with a French family where he sharpened his language skills well enough to deserve appointment, in 1800, to a committee to translate a journal written by American envoys to France.

The most interesting and common features found in letters he received as senator had to do with repeated requests for help in getting government jobs, appeals for higher salaries for public servants, and protests against the tax on spirits.

His first wife, Lydia, died in 1801. He married Esther Millard, the daughter of a minister, in 1803. They had five children. His closing years were among his most useful, for he collected and preserved historical materials and assembled data for a history of the state, though he did not live to finish the project. He never lost his interest in education and actively pursued learning until the day he died at age seventy-six. He was buried at Swan Point Cemetery near Foster.

JOSEPH STANTON

July 19, 1739 *September 22, 1823*

Joseph Stanton is the least known member of the first Senate. He is not listed in standard reference works. Even Senator Maclay, of Pennsylvania, fails to mention him.

It is odd because he was not born of an itinerant or poor family. He comes from a long line of well-to-do Stantons. He was born in Charlestown, Rhode Island, the fifth generation of the family in New England. His great-great-grandfather was an important trader and a master of Indian languages from whom succeeding generations inherited huge amounts of lands.

When Joseph was twenty years old in 1759 he served in the French and Indian War as a second lieutenant in the expedition against Canada. For six years, from 1768 to 1774, he was a member of the Colonial House of Representatives. When the revolution began he was on the committee of safety and entered the service as a colonel in one of the Rhode Island regiments. He reached the rank of colonel in the revolutionary army and served with distinction.

His community sent him to the state convention considering ratification of the Constitution in 1790. He was not enamored of the document but voted for it when it became apparent that staying out of the Union would be too costly and impracticable. He was elected to the Senate, drew the four-year term, and returned home when it expired in 1793. He was still popular with his constituents and after Senate service he was sent to the lower house of the state assembly for several terms and to the federal House of Representatives from 1801 to 1807.

Letters addressed to him in the Senate carry the title General, which could have been earned after the revolution but was more likely honorary. Copies of several letters that he sent to constituents or friends express a strong aversion to slavery, but since he owned forty slaves and was a politician, it is impossible to know his true sentiments. He was well-educated, comfortable in any society and very wealthy with large land holdings. Toward the end of his life his wealth and estates dropped in value as he failed to keep up with rapidly changing business practices.

He died in his home in Charlestown, Rhode Island, at age sixty-eight and was interred in the family cemetery.

SOUTH CAROLINA

PIERCE BUTLER

July 11, 1744   *February 15, 1822*

Pierce Butler was born in Ireland in 1744, the third son of Sir Richard Butler, Baronet. Young Pierce entered the British army at an unusually early age. Through the influence of his family he was commissioned a lieutenant by his eleventh birthday. By 1766, at age twenty-two, he was a major stationed in Boston. Eventually he switched sides. On January 10, 1771 he married Mary Middleton, daughter of a land owning army colonel in South Carolina. In 1773, he made the decision to settle permanently in America. As was customary in aristocratic families, once he decided to became a farmer and politician in America, he sold his commission.

Though he was not involved in military activity he held several political positions, many simultaneously, during the revolution. From 1778 to 1782, and again from 1784 to 1789, he was a representative in the state legislature. In 1779 he was also state adjutant general. Likewise, in 1786, he served on the commission to fix (determine exactly) disputed state boundaries and in March 1787 was elected a delegate to the Confederation Congress.

Butler posed as the champion of the small farmers and pioneers of the back country. He supported their economic and political program for reform, for relocation of the state capital, for a better system of representation, for revaluing property and for reforming taxes. He was chosen to represent the state at the Constitutional Convention in Philadelphia.

At the Convention he was a consistent supporter of Hamilton's economic and political position and was vigorous in advocacy of a strong central government. He believed that only those who owned property should be counted when determining a state's population for representation. He authored the infamous fugitive slave clause in the Constitution. Although he was not a member of the state ratification convention he worked hard for adoption of the Constitution.

In 1789 he was elected to the United States Senate and drew the two-year term. He voted for Hamilton's funding bill and for the assumption of state debts but opposed the tariff and the Judiciary Act. His position on the tariff is understandable since it would hurt the economic interests of South Carolina. On very narrow self-interest grounds, he voted against the Judiciary Act which established the federal court system. The terms of the Judiciary Act as written would have placed appointments to the court in the hands of people who were not sympathetic to Butler's political views.

The proponents of a strong military could count on his unswerving support, and he worked hard for higher pay for senators. He wanted to limit the power of the president to remove officers but only because he was piqued at Washington at the time. He seemed to hate Pennsylvania because he hated Quakers and he hated Quakers because they were opposed to slavery.

His Senate votes were unpredictable, as they depended upon his feelings at the moment and on his perception of the effect on his interests. Butler was very ambitious but without the intelligence to achieve his goals. He was impulsive, often quite explosive in his reactions and he frequently put forth contradictory positions. He was reelected but resigned in 1796 because he intended to become a candidate for the governorship. At the last minute, for no apparent reason, he refused to allow his name to be put forward. In 1802 he was elected for the last time to fill an unexpired term in the Senate. There he railed against the twelfth amendment to the Constitution, accusing the Jeffersonian Republicans of abusing their power as the Federalist's had done before them. Again he resigned before the term ended in 1808 and this time he retired permanently.

William Pierce, of Georgia, wrote that Butler was a very vain man with a huge fortune and that, inexplicably, he somehow maintained his popularity at home. Senator Maclay reported that his language was excessive and abusive and often pointless. He was a difficult man to work with and a difficult man to like.

He died in Philadelphia and was buried in St. Michael's Church in Charlestown, South Carolina.

RALPH IZARD

January 23, 1741 *May 30, 1804*

Ralph Izard was born to a family that was part of the cultured, comfortable and assured society that dominated rice and indigo production in the Carolinas and Georgia. They were firmly established in land, money, slaves, social position and influence. When Ralph was seven his father died and as the only surviving son, he inherited all his father's holdings. At the age of twelve, he entered school at Hackney, England and then Cambridge, from which he graduated in 1763.

He spent time in South Carolina but more often he was in New York City pursuing Alice De Lancey. She was the daughter of Peter De Lancey, a member of the New York Assembly from what is now The Bronx, and the niece of James De Lancey, a former chief justice and lieutenant governor of New York. Her parents owned a valuable sawmill and gristmill, as well as a large estate in The Bronx. The young couple were married in May 1767. During the next few years most of Izard's time was spent in New York City. His plantations were run by overseers. In 1771 the Izards bought a house in London and participated in the social whirl of the very wealthy. The revolutionary events from 1763 to 1776 passed the Izards without notice.

In 1775, when fighting had already occurred in the colonies, they went to Paris with the purpose of returning to America. They were still there in 1777, when Izard arranged, with the help of friends in the second Continental Congress, to be appointed commissioner to Tuscany. Since the government of Tuscany never arranged to receive him, he remained in Paris. He asserted that, as a diplomat, he had a right to participate in negotiations with the French court. Benjamin Franklin did not agree with that position and blocked Izard from any participation. Consequently, Izard developed a passionate hatred for Franklin. Izard also contended that he should not have to pay duties on any purchases and that he should be paid a salary as minister to Tuscany out of funds collected in France.

While in Paris his South Carolina estates were sequestered and his wife's brother, James, and her uncle Oliver De Lancey, became infamous Loyalist leaders in New York. Suspicion about Izard's loyalty spread. He sent his resignation to Congress but before it reached there he was recalled to face an investigation. Upon his arrival he met with Washington and during the course of the meeting Izard claims that he advised him to place General Nathaniel Greene in command of the southern army. There is no evidence available to corroborate this claim. After his dispatches were examined he was exonerated.

South Carolina sent him as a delegate to the Confederation Congress from 1782 until peace was established in 1783. During this time he pledged his estates as security for the purchase of ships in Europe. When offered the nomination for governor he declined. He did serve several years in the state legislature. After ratification of the Constitution he was elected to the Senate and drew the six-year term. He served from 1789 until 1795 when he retired from public life. He was a strong supporter of the president. He voted for Hamilton's financial program and in favor of all military bills and for higher pay for senators. Surprisingly, he voted to change a bill which would have recognized the president's power to remove appointees. His positions and reasoning were often obscure. Like his colleague Pierce, he hated Quakers, Franklin, slavery opponents, and Pennsylvania. When Adams held forth on the necessity of titles and in favor of displays of pomp Izard coined the fitting phrase for Adams, "His Rotundity." In the third Congress he was elected president *pro tempore.*

Izard was no believer in democracy. He was sure of his own superiority and of his right to govern. As he got older he became more irascible and short tempered. It has been suggested that his violent and explosive temper was caused by his high blood pressure and gout.

He died at age sixty-two and is buried outside the church of St. James, in Goose Creek, South Carolina.

VIRGINIA

WILLIAM GRAYSON

?, 1736   *March 12, 1790*

    Grayson's father emigrated from Scotland to Virginia, where he married Susannah Monroe, an aunt of James Monroe. Their son William played a creditable role in the Revolution. Grayson was tutored at home before being sent to the College of Philadelphia where he studied law. He established a practice in the area surrounding Prince William County, Virginia and in a few years gained a respectable following and financial success. He married Eleanor Smallwood, a local woman with a small inheritance.

    In response to the Intolerable Acts of 1774 an independent company of cadets was organized in his county and Grayson was elected captain. In 1776 he was appointed aide-de-camp to Washington. Early in 1777 he was promoted to colonel and placed in charge of a regiment he had organized. He showed such great courage and leadership skills in the Battle of Monmouth that in spring 1778 Washington appointed him to meet with General

William Howe for an exchange of prisoners. The following year, Grayson resigned from the army and accepted an appointment as commissioner on the Board of War. After the battle of Yorktown he returned to his neglected law practice and became active in local and state politics.

He was elected to the Virginia House of Delegates for two years, 1784-85 and reelected for another year in 1788. During the two intervening years, 1786 and 1787, he was a representative to the Confederation Congress. Grayson had a deep interest in the development of the newly acquired western lands, and participated in the debates over the Northwest Ordinance. He supported its anti-slavery clause as a necessary concession to popular opinion in the north and east.

He actively opposed the ratification of the Constitution chiefly because he believed that the proposed government would not make navigation of the Mississippi any safer. His sincere and consistent position for popular control of weak, limited government, and his recognition of the necessity for a Bill of Rights made him acceptable to the antifederalist Virginia legislature. He wanted a weak federal judiciary and preferred to restrict the power of federal courts to admiralty and maritime cases. He opposed all pretentious and monarchical titles and all imposts as being unjust and oppressive. He was elected to the Senate and took his seat on May 21, 1789.

Grayson was in poor health by the time he reached the Senate and did not serve out the two-year term that he drew. The steady deterioration in his health caused him to seek a leave of absence which was granted on August 6.

Friends said that he loved to debate and to use his mental powers. Many have noted his refined manners, his humor and his wit. Grayson County, in Virginia, is named for him. Seven months after he took his leave he became the first sitting senator to die. It happened in Dumphries, Virginia and interment was on the nearby family estate, Belle Air.

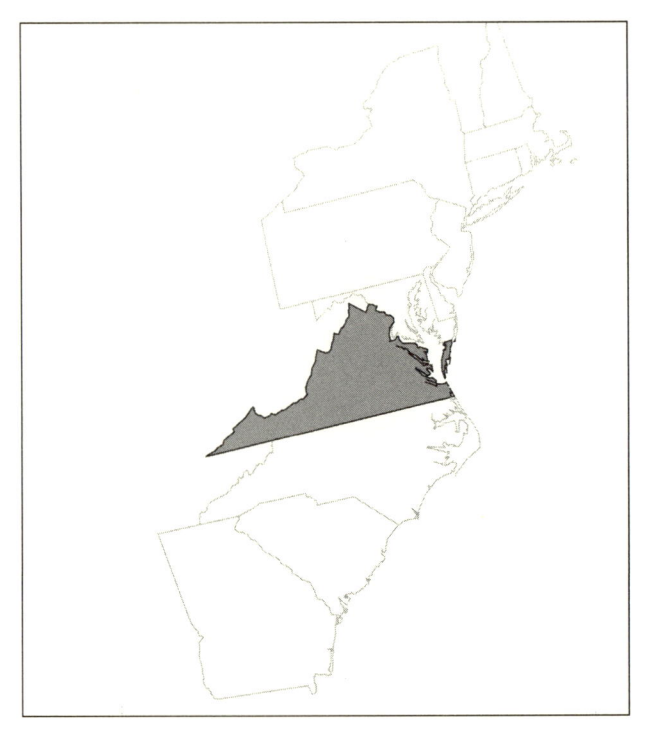

JOHN WALKER

February 13, 1744　　　　　　　　　　*December 2, 1809*

By the time of John Walker's birth in 1744, at Castle Hill, in Albemarle County, Virginia, the Walker family had accumulated large landholdings. His mother's family was equally prosperous. His grandmother was a sister of George Washington. His father had served as commissary general for the Virginia troops in Braddock's army and as a commissioner to deal with the Indians at Fort Stanwix, New York. For years his father served in the House of Burgesses and was president of the commission that fixed the boundary between North Carolina and Virginia. The father was determined that his son would have the education necessary to carry on in this tradition of civic involvement.

After finishing his education in 1766 John moved to Belvoir, in Albemarle County, and began to enjoy the life of a prosperous planter on his share of family land. He married Elizabeth Moore and they had one daughter.

During the revolution John and his father were commissioned to negotiate a peaceful settlement of differences with the Indians in the Pittsburgh area. For some time young Walker served on Washington's staff with the rank of colonel. Washington reported that he was a man of prudence and honor and that he had the ability to assume positions of responsibility. Washington's letter of recommendation to Patrick Henry was instrumental in securing a position in the Virginia state government for him. A close friendship developed between Henry and Walker which led to a lifetime of political collaboration. At the end of the war, Walker returned to farm management but remained active in local political life. Thus it was that Governor Henry appointed Walker the temporary replacement to the seat left vacant by Grayson's death.

Walker took the oath of office on April 26, 1790 and served for nine months until James Monroe was elected by the Legislature of Virginia to complete the term. Walker did not contribute to the debates in the Senate but was on record as favoring the Potomac River site for the nation's permanent capital. He attended regularly but was a quiet observer.

He died at age sixty-five, in Madison Mills, Virginia. Interment was in the family cemetery on the Belvoir estate near Cismont.

JAMES MONROE

April 28, 1758 *July 4, 1831*

James Monroe, born to a simple and quiet family, received his first education from his parents. From 1769 until he started college Monroe attended the academy of Reverend Archibald Campbell. Monroe became an orphan at sixteen and was placed with his uncle, Joseph Jones. By mutual agreement Jones sold the family farm in 1774 and Monroe entered William and Mary College. In 1776 when Monroe was a senior the college closed because of the revolution.

He joined the Virginia Third Regiment and fought in the battles of Harlem Heights, White Plains, and Trenton, where he was wounded. In the campaigns of 1777-78 he served as aide to Lord Sterling with the rank of major and saw further action at Germantown, Brandywine, and Monmouth. He was an authentic war hero. His promotion to major removed him from the Continental Army and he had difficulty finding a place in the state forces. His uncle urged him to apprentice in law under Thomas Jefferson.

He stayed with Jefferson until 1783 when he was elected to the Confederation Congress. In 1788 Jefferson designed Monroe's first home, Ashlawn, originally called Highland. It was located across the valley from Jefferson's Monticello, and it cost Monroe $3000 to build. Monroe maintained that home from 1799 until he built a home at Oak Hill, in northern Virginia, in 1826. Their friendship continued until Jefferson's death.

He served in the Confederation Congress for three years. At that time in his life he was unsure of himself and was sometimes in awe of figures with more poise and family recognition. Uncomfortable in social situations, he was introspective and solemn rather than frivolous or lighthearted. In February 1786 he married the beautiful and well-educated Elizabeth Kortright. His term in Congress expired that year and after attending the Annapolis Convention the newlyweds returned to Fredericksburg, Virginia, where Monroe intended to practice law. They had two daughters.

He was not sent to the Constitutional Convention in Philadelphia but was elected to the state ratification convention. He aligned himself with Patrick Henry and the forces opposing the adoption of the Constitution. He said that he feared the Constitution had been given too great a concentration of power.

In fall 1788 Monroe ran for the House of Representatives against James Madison. It was a serious political mistake and he was badly beaten. When William Grayson died and a special senatorial election was called for December 1790, Monroe saw his chance, campaigned for the position and won. On December 6, 1790 he took the seat vacated by John Walker, who had been appointed to fill in for William Grayson.

During his first year in the Senate, Monroe was often a critic of Washington. He actively opposed the appointment of John Jay as envoy to England and of Gouverneur Morris as minister to France. He opposed the National Bank bill and was an opponent of Hamilton's financial program as well as of all efforts to strengthen the federal government.

He was reelected to the Senate in 1792 but resigned in 1794 to accept Washington's offer of an appointment as minister to France. The years from 1796 until his death were filled with personal and political triumphs including election as president of the United States.

When he finished his presidency he retired to his home, Oak

Hill, and stayed until poverty and ill-health made it unwise to remain alone. After the death of his wife in May 1830 he moved to the home of his daughter and son-in-law in New York City.

Except for two years practicing law in Fredericksburg he held government positions throughout his life. He was the first man to earn his entire livelihood on the government payroll. He was a very ordinary man in almost every way, neither a scholarly intellectual nor an imaginative innovator. Lacking any gift as an orator, he could not move people or inspire them to action. He was never praised for great compassion, or grace in speech, or insight into human nature. He earned praise for his good judgment in foreign affairs and his ability to reflect the nation's will.

He died on the Fourth of July 1831 and was buried in the new Marble cemetery on Second Street and Second Avenue in New York City. At the request of Virginia his body was exhumed in late June 1858 and reinterred in Holywood cemetery in Richmond.

RICHARD HENRY LEE
January 20, 1732 *June 19, 1794*

Richard Henry Lee was the seventh of Thomas Lee and Hannah Ludwell's eleven children. The Lees were successful land owners and lived in a mansion, called Stratford, located in Westmoreland County, Virginia. Early instruction for Richard, as it was for all the children, was by private tutor and his finishing education was in Wakefield Academy in Yorkshire. After graduation he toured Europe for a few months, returning home in 1752. Most of his ancestors had been active in political life and he followed the same path. He began public service as a justice of the peace in 1757 and entered the House of Burgesses a year later.

In that same year he married Anne Aylett, daughter of a neighboring landowner. They established their own residence calling it Chantilly, where they had two sons and two daughters. When his first wife died in 1768 he remarried and had two more daughters.

Within a few years Lee became an influential member of the House of Burgesses. He moved into leadership as the defender of colonial rights when England imposed taxes in 1764. He authored two petitions protesting the stamp duties, one of which went to the king and the other to the House of Lords. Early in the struggle he saw the necessity for united action and suggested the idea of committees of correspondence, which did not begin to function fully until 1773. He was an active member of the Non-Importation Committee for Virginia and led the protest against the rule which allowed Admiralty courts to take away trial by jury. When the Intolerable Acts were passed and the port of Boston was closed he proposed a meeting of a general congress to act for all the colonies. He became a delegate to the first Continental Congress in 1774 and served on its leading committees. However, it was at the second Continental Congress where he was most influential.

It was Lee's motion which led to the Declaration of Independence. He was one of the four men in the first Senate to sign that document. He stayed active in Congress until 1779 at which time he decided he could be more effective in Virginia. When he returned to the Confederation Congress in 1784 he was unanimously elected its president.

He was fearful of granting the power of the purse and the sword to Congress. This won him support and he was chosen as a delegate to the Constitutional Convention. However, he did not accept the appointment.

He employed his talents against the ratification of the Constitution on the grounds that it lacked a Bill of Rights and gave away too much power. Once Virginia ratified the Constitution he was elected to the first Senate.

Lee supported the idea of giving titles to Washington and Adams. He switched positions several times on issues involving use of American vessels in the tea trade and on the tariff. He was consistent in voting against a standing army and for maintaining the power of state courts on federal issues. To force Rhode Island to ratify the Constitution a bill was proposed which placed exorbitant charges on all her trade while she remained outside the Union. Lee took a principled stand against using such forceful tactics. He labored diligently to get the Bill of Rights adopted in the Senate.

In spite of their differences Senator Maclay said that while Lee had some ambition and vainglory he had a clear head and great experience, and that he always sought to serve the public. Though Lee sometimes expended considerable unwarranted energy on minor issues, most of his efforts were devoted to the betterment of mankind. He was almost as good an orator as Patrick Henry.

He resigned his Senate seat in October 1792 worn out by his labors. He died at his estate after two short years of retirement, much too young at fifty-eight. Interment was in the family burial ground at Mount Pleasant near Hague, Westmoreland County, Virginia.

The First Senate in Profile

A profile of the first Senate shows that of the twenty-nine members, fifteen served as officers, or in some other capacity, in the Revolutionary army; twenty had state legislative experience; twenty-one were elected to the first or second Continental Congress or to the Confederation Congress and nineteen of them served; nineteen attended college or had equivalent schooling; twelve members served in the Constitutional Convention; fourteen were elected to the state constitutional ratifying conventions, and two more worked very hard and successfully to get the necessary votes to approve the document; four signed the Declaration of Independence, two of whom joined another seven making a total of nine who signed the Constitution; only George Read and Robert Morris had the triple distinction of signing both the Declaration of Independence and the United States Constitution, as well as serving as members in the first Senate; twenty-two were Federalists who supported the Hamiltonian program with some individuals opposing one or another proposal for local political or for personal reasons. William Grayson, Samuel Johnston, Richard Henry Lee, William Maclay, James Monroe were antifederalists and Joseph Stanton was opposed to concentrated power but voted in ways that make it hard to pinpoint his political orientation.

Five of them were given federal executive offices after their Senate service. King and Monroe became ambassadors to England and France respectively. Ellsworth became Chief Justice of the United States and special envoy to France. Paterson was appointed Associate Justice of the Supreme Court. Hawkins was appointed by Washington, first as a federal negotiator with the Creek Confederacy, then as federal agent to the Creeks and finally as General Superintendent of Indian Tribes south of the Ohio River.

The oldest, William Samuel Johnson, was sixty-one, the youngest was James Monroe at thirty-one. The average age was forty-seven. Eighteen were lawyers or had legal training of some kind, though not all practiced. For example, Theodore Foster studied law but never practiced. He did little work of any kind, living on his family wealth while pursuing his antiquarian interests. James Monroe practiced law for two years, and otherwise earned his living entirely from government positions.

Several may be classified as businessmen/financiers, but Robert Morris was in a class by himself in terms of the amount of money involved in his transactions. John Langdon was a businessman, being, at various times, a shipper, a merchant, a sea captain, and later a money lender and investor.

Paine Wingate was the only clergyman and Jonathan Elmer was the only medical doctor. One man, Benjamin Hawkins, stands out because he had a classical education, mastered several languages, and spent his life in the service of the American Indian. There were many men who could be classified as landowners and/or farmers. Such a designation may be misleading, for with the exception of William Few, none of them physically planted and harvested. The people who fall in this category are Paine Wingate, Philemon Dickinson, William Few, William Maclay, Pierce Butler, William Grayson and John Walker.

Ralph Izard can properly be described as a playboy and dilettante, as well as a large landowner. Thirteen owned slaves, some only one or two and only for a short time.

There were those in the first Senate who knew that the judgment of history and the future welfare and survival of the new country could rest upon their personal decisions. Every action and every debate or discussion by these men shows their serious purpose and deep concern. Men like Oliver Ellsworth, William Maclay, George Read, John Langdon, and Richard Henry Lee certainly fit in this category.

A few people suggested that Pierce Butler was unbalanced because of his extreme language and frequent accusations against those who disagreed with him.

There were others, however, who used the Senate exclusively to further their own ambitions, or, in one case, to enjoy the city and have a good time. Many used their knowledge about Hamilton's financial plans to make large sums of money. Today we would call that action a misuse of insider information, and such conduct unethical, maybe illegal — offering sufficient grounds for an investigation by the Justice Department.

Several were there because they had nothing better to do, or because they did not get their first choice of a government position. There was a widely held belief that the states were the real centers of power, and that one who had political ambitions would do well to seek those offices. Therefore, the Senate did not attract some of the best talent around. They could, instead, be found in state governments.

The first Senate was not a fixed group of individuals. First, there were the changes wrought by the three sessions drawn by lot, including those who were, or were not reelected. In addition, there were those newly elected as well as those who, in the midst of things, took leave, or even resigned, for various reasons such as accepting appointments, or for family and business obligations, or ill health. Still others were appointed to fill those unexpired terms, and some of those replacements were themselves, replaced at election time. This constant changeover required some flexibility on the part of all the members.

Knowing, as we do, what committees and bureaucracy can sometimes do to projects, it is remarkable that such a potpourri of signers, resigners, absentees, attendees, appointees, the selfish, the selfless, and the like could produce anything worthwhile. Of the good, the bad, and the indifferent in that cross section of humanity, there was enough of the good present, so that, on balance, the first Senate met its responsibilities. It surely did well enough to allow the new government to get its bearings and its footings. After all, that government stands today.

Profile Reference Chart

NAME	STATE	Revolutionary Army	State Legislature	Continental and Federation Congress	College or equal	Constitutional Convention	State ratification or work for it	Signed Declaration and/or Constitution	Federalist	Age	Slaves	Executive Branch Service
Richard Bassett	DE	Y	Y		Y	Y	Y	Constitution	Y	44	Y	
Pierce Butler	SC		Y	3		Y	W	Constitution	Y	45	Y	
Charles Carroll of Carrollton	MD		Y	2	Y	Y	Y	Declaration	Y	52	Y	
Tristram Dalton	MA		Y		Y	Y	Y		Y	51	Y	
Philemon Dickinson	NJ	Y		3	Y				Y	50		
Oliver Ellsworth	CT		Y			Y	YW		Y	44		
Jonathan Elmer	NJ	Y	Y		Y		Y		Y	44		
William Few	GA	Y	Y			Y	Y	Constitution	Y	41	Y	
Theodore Foster	RI		Y				YW		Y	37		
William Grayson	VA	Y	Y							53	Y	
James Gunn	GA	Y		5					Y	50	Y	
Benjamin Hawkins	NC	Y		3	Y				Y	35	Y	
John Henry	MD		Y	2-3	Y				Y	39		
Ralph Izard	SC		Y	3	Y				Y	48	Y	
William Samuel Johnson	CT		Y	3	Y	Y		Constitution	Y	61		
Samuel Johnston	NC		Y	1-2-3	Y		Y		Y	56	Y	
Rufus King	NY	Y	Y	3-5	Y	Y	Y	Constitution	Y	34		Y
John Langdon	NH	Y	Y	2-3		Y	Y	Constitution	Y	48		
Richard Henry Lee	VA			1-2-3				Declaration		57	Y	
William Maclay	PA	Y	Y							55		
James Monroe	VA			3	Y		Y			32		Y
Robert Morris	PA		Y	2		Y		BOTH	Y	55		
William Paterson	NJ	Y	Y		Y	Y		Constitution	Y	44		Y
George Read	DE		Y	1-2-3		Y	Y	BOTH	Y	55	Y	
Philip Schuyler	NY	Y		3					Y	56		
Joseph Stanton	RI	Y		4	Y	Y	Y		Y	50		
Caleb Strong	MA		Y		Y		Y		Y	44		
John Walker	VA	Y								45	Y	
Paine Wingate	NH		Y	3	Y		Y.		Y	50		

1 = 1st Continental Congress; 2 = 2nd Continental Congress; 3 = Confederation Congress
4 = House of Representatives; 5 = Elected, but did not serve;
Y = Was a member; W = Worked hard in some way to pass.

NOTES ON THE BILL OF RIGHTS

With the great advantage of hindsight it is easy to see that the addition of the Bill of Rights to the Constitution was the single most important accomplishment of the first Congress. To understand the role played by the Senate in the passage of the Bill of Rights, a brief review of why and how the Bill arrived in Congress is helpful.

In a speech to the Constitutional Convention on September 12, 1787, George Mason, author of the Virginia Declaration of Rights, stated that a Bill of Rights should be included in the Constitution. Unfortunately Mason's proposal came after months of difficult work, and five days before adjournment, when delegates were in no mood to prolong their deliberations. Mason cleverly pointed out that by using the Declarations of Rights found in every state constitution, a Bill of Rights for the federal constitution could be written in a few hours since a consensus existed as to the rights which needed constitutional guarantees. A motion to that effect was made by Elbridge Gerry, but it was unanimously defeated by the states voting as units.

Two opposing points of view developed in reaction to Mason's proposal. Roger Sherman presented the view that the Constitution did not repeal any of the state guarantees, nor did it give the government any power to infringe upon those rights. The opposing view, expressed by Richard Henry Lee and others, held that under Article VI, the Constitution was the supreme law of the land and that any state laws in conflict had to give way. Furthermore, all state judges were bound by an oath to obey the federal law. Since the new government was decidedly stronger, they held that a Bill of Rights was absolutely essential. There were two attempts to resolve this problem by including a Bill of Rights in the Constitution prior to submission to the states. Neither attempt received support.

Immediately after the Constitution was offered to the states for ratification, a debate about a Bill of Rights began. Hundreds of pamphlets, addresses, articles, newspaper accounts, letters and memorials (petitions) poured into the public debate. The rights issue became the focus of contention. The Antifederalists, those against adopting the Constitution, asserted that the absence of such a bill was a fatal flaw. The Federalists, those favoring adoption, argued that a Bill of Rights was unnecessary. Madison promised the Virginia ratifying convention that a Bill of Rights would be added after adoption. In order to secure adoption, Federalists in other states made similar commitments.

According to Article V, a two-thirds vote of each house of Congress is required to propose amendments, and then these proposed amendments require approval by three-fourths of the states to be ratified. When the first Congress began meeting, the need for a Bill of Rights seemed, for many, to be less important than passing a tax law or setting tariff fees in order to get the new government functioning. Madison, sitting in the House of Representatives, fulfilled his promise when he submitted amendments based on the recommendations of state ratifying conventions, on June 8, 1789. The House voted approval of seventeen amendments on August 24, which were then sent to the Senate for action.

Until February 1794, the meetings of the Senate were secret. Consequently there is no record available which would allow a reasoned judgment on the roles played by the various Senators. The material found in the Senate *Journal*, and in the *Annals of Congress*, is very limited, and deals only with the attempts to delete or add amendments, or to make changes in wording. Senator Maclay was present when the amendments were introduced, but was absent, due to illness during the debates. He reported that Senators Izard, Langdon, and Morris treated them contemptuously. Izard moved that they should be postponed until the next session, Langdon seconded, and they were supported by Morris in an angry, but ineffective, speech.

Lee, with the support of Grayson, worked hard to gain Senate approval for prompt consideration. The Izard motion lost, and the Senate debated the House-approved amendments from September 2, to September 9, when the changed version was returned to the House. Essentially, the Senate improved the quality of the language by striking out verbiage, eliminating some provisions, combining similar or related provisions, and cutting the number of amendments to fourteen.

To reconcile differences between the House and Senate versions, a conference committee was formed. The Senate members were Oliver Ellsworth, Charles Carroll, and William Paterson. Once the work of reconciliation was completed, the final versions were returned to the House and Senate for action. Ellsworth made the conference report for the Senate, which promptly concurred in the changes. The President transmitted the amendments to the states for their action on October 2, 1789. It took two years, until December 15, 1791, to achieve state ratification. Finally, on March 1, 1792, Secretary of State Thomas Jefferson sent notice to state governors that three-fourths of the states had ratified ten amendments and that they were now part of the Constitution.

The Senators in the Order in which the States Ratified the Constitution

DELAWARE
 Richard Bassett - March 4, 1789 - March 3, 1793
 George Read - March 4, 1789 - Reelected 1791 - Resigned 1793

PENNSYLVANIA
 William Maclay - March 4, 1789 - March 3, 1791
 Robert Morris - March 4, 1789 - March 3, 1795

NEW JERSEY
 Jonathan Elmer - March 4, 1789 - March 3, 1791
 William Paterson - March 4, 1789 - Resigned November 13, 1790
 Philemon Dickinson - Elected to Paterson's vacated seat December 6, 1790 - March 3, 1793

GEORGIA
 William Few - March 4, 1789 - March 3, 1793
 James Gunn - March 4, 1789 - March 3, 1800

CONNECTICUT
 Oliver Ellsworth - March 4, 1789 - Reelected March 3, 1791 - Resigned 1796
 William Samuel Johnson - March 4, 1789 - Resigned 1792

MASSACHUSETTS
 Tristram Dalton - March 4, 1789 - March 3, 1792
 Caleb Strong - March 4, 1789 - Reelected 1795 - Resigned 1796

MARYLAND
 Charles Carroll of Carrollton - March 4, 1789 - Resigned November 1792
 John Henry - March 3, 1789 - Reelected 1795 - Resigned December 10, 1797

Senators in Order in which States Ratified Constitution / 131

SOUTH CAROLINA
    Pierce Butler - March 4, 1789 - Reelected March 1791 -
        Resigned 1796
    Ralph Izard - March 4, 1789 - March 3, 1795
NEW HAMPSHIRE
    John Langdon - March 4, 1789 - Reelected 1795 -
        Retired March 3, 1801
    Paine Wingate - March 4, 1789 - March 3, 1793
VIRGINIA
    Richard Henry Lee - April 6, 1789 - resigned October 22, 1792
    William Grayson - May 21, 1789 - sick leave, August 6, 1789 -
        Died March 12, 1790
    John Walker - replaced Grayson - April 26, 1790 -
        December 6, 1790
    James Monroe - Elected to Grayson's seat - December 6, 1790 -
        Reelected March 3, 1792 - Resigned - 1794
NEW YORK
    Rufus King - July 25, 1789 - Reelected March 3, 1795 -
        Resigned 1796
    Philip Schuyler - July 16, 1789 - March 3, 1791
NORTH CAROLINA
    Benjamin Hawkins - November 1789 - Sworn, January 13, 1790
        - March 3, 1795
    Samuel Johnston - January 29, 1790 - March 3, 1793
RHODE ISLAND
    Theodore Foster - Elected May 1790 - Sworn June 25, 1790
        Reelected March 1791, 1797 and March 1813
    Joseph Stanton - Elected May 1790 - Sworn June 25, 1790 -
        March 3, 1793

CHRONOLOGY

1754 Benjamin Franklin proposes the Albany Plan of Union, for colonial unity. Models it on the structure and process of the Iroquois Confederacy.

1774 September 5 to October 26 - The First Continental Congress composed of representatives from most of the colonies deliberates for seven weeks. Not a legislative body. Designed to share views in the hope of finding sufficient agreement for unified action.

1775 May 10 - The Second Continental Congress meets in Philadelphia. All thirteen colonies represented. This is the government of the United States until 1781. Select George Washington to head the military forces to defend Boston. Richard Henry Lee moves for Independence June 7, Jefferson writes Declaration of independence. Create a plan for a new government, the Articles of Confederation. (Not adopted until 1781). Thirteen independent states join for common action in dealing with their problems - a league of friendship. No president, no power of taxation, no national court.

1781 The Articles of Confederation adopted.

1781-1789 Government of the United States.

1787 May 25 to September 17 - Constitutional Convention.

Washington elected to preside over the Constitutional Convention. He and thirty-eight others signed.

1788 June 21 - New Hampshire becomes the ninth state to ratify the Constitution of the United States of America which becomes the law of the land.

June 26 - Virginia and New York ratify the Constitution.

1789 The following dates were set by the Articles of Confederation Congress:
1. January, 1789 - the first Wednesday - to select presidential electors.
2. March 4 - for the new Congress to assemble.

Federal Hall, in New York City (Formerly Town Hall) site of First and Second Sessions.

March 4 - 1st session supposed to begin — (NO quorum, no session).

April 1 - The House of Representatives achieves its quorum.

April 6 - Senate achieves quorum, first session begins. Elect officers. President of the Senate, John Adams. President *Pro Tempore*, Senator John Langdon, New Hampshire.

April 21 - Vice-President John Adams assumes the chair as President of the Senate.

Arrange lottery for dividing up Senators into two, four, and six year terms.

May 15 - Twenty senators present draw lots from a lottery.

July - New York State Legislature finally elects their senators, who missed the opening sessions.

August 26 - Compensation Bill passes, the first to provide senators a salary of six dollars per day.

September 29 - 1st session ends.

1790 January 4 - 2nd session begins.

August 12 - 2nd session ends.

Congress will move from New York City.

December 6 - 3rd session begins in Philadelphia. The first Congress opens its third session in the Senate chamber of Congress Hall, the new county court house. Remains here ten years.

1791 March 3 - 3rd session ends.

The terms of those in Class 1 (two years) expire at the end of the first Congress in March.

1793 March 3 - The terms of those in Class 2 (four years) ends for the second Congress.

1795 March 3 - Third Congress ends. End of terms for those in third class, who served the full six years.

1800 The government moves to the new capital, Washington, D.C. For the next ten years, the Senate meets in small quarters on the ground floor of the new Capitol building, since the rest of the building is not yet finished.

1810 The Senate meets in the chamber located on the second floor of the north wing of the completed Capitol.

1812 War between The United States and Great Britain

1814 August - British burn the Capitol building. Senate moves to a small, plain residence one block away.

1819 Restoration of the burned Capitol completed. Senate settles into its permanent home.

1833 Fire destroys Federal Hall, in New York City.

1861-1864-on During the Civil War, the original dome is replaced by a soaring cast iron dome weighing almost seven million pounds. Manufacturer: The Janes and Beebe Ironworks located in what will be The Bronx.

Notes

[1] See "First Senate Meeting Dates and Other Data," page 18 for lottery results.

[2] atrabilious - melancholic or hypochondriac; *parvanimous* - not a recognized word. Apparently coined from parvanimity which means the quality of smallness of mind or spirit; meanness, the opposite of the noun magnanimity, generous of spirit, not petty. However, the adverb magnanimous does not have the corresponding antonym parvanimous, clever though it may be; magna=large, parvu=small, animus=mind or spirit.

[3] Forerunner of Princeton University. See page 21.

[4] See page 18.

[5] See page 18.

[6] Forerunner of Princeton University. See page 21.

[7] See page 18.

[8] Forerunner of Princeton University. See page 21.

[9] See page 18.

BIBLIOGRAPHY

Annals of The Congress of the United States. Washington, D.C. Gales & Seaton. 1834-1856. Proceedings from 1789-1824.

Baker, Richard Allen. *The Senate of the United States: A Bicentennial History.* Malabar, Florida. Robert E. Krieger Publishing Company. 1988.

Brown, William Garrott. *The Life of Oliver Ellsworth.* New York. Da Capo Press, 1970.

Chitwood, Oliver P. *Richard H. Lee: Statesman of the Revolution.* Morgantown. West Virginia Library. 1967.

Deas, Anne Izard. ed. *Correspondence of Mr. Ralph Izard of South Carolina, From the Year 1774 to 1804. With a Short Memoir.* New York. C.S. Francis & Company. 1844.

Ernst, Robert. *Rufus King: American Federalist.* Chapel Hill. University of North Carolina Press. 1968.

Fribourg, Marjorie G. *The U.S. Congress: Men Who Steered Its Course. 1789-1867.* Philadelphia: M. Smith Company. 1972.

Groce, George C.,Jr. *William Samuel Johnson: A Maker of the Constitution.* New York. Columbia University Press. 1937.

Lettieri, Ronald John. *Connecticut's Young Man of the Revolution: Oliver Ellsworth.* Hartford. American Revolution Bicentennial Commission of Connecticut, 1978.

Read, William T. *Life and Correspondence of George Read.* Philadelphia. J.B. Lippencott and Company. 1870.

Reid, T. R. *Congressional Odyssey: The Story of a Senate Bill.* San Francisco. W.H. Freeman & Company. 1980.

Ritchie, Donald A. *Know Your Government: The Senate.* New York. Chelsea House Publishers. 1985.

Maclay, Edgar S., ed. *The Journal of William Maclay.* Harrisburg New York. Albert & Charles Boni. 1927.

Tuckerman, Bayard. *Life of General Philip Schuyler.* Freeport, New York. 1969.

Reference Works

Appletons Encyclopedia of American Biography.
Biographical Directory of American Congress.
Dictionary of American Biography.
Drake Dictionary of American Biography.
Enyclopaedia of American Biography.
National Cyclopaedia of American Biography.
The 20th Century Biographical Dictionary of American Notables.

Portrait Credits

John Adams — *Gilbert and Jane Stuart; The National Portrait Gallery.*
Oliver Ellsworth — *David Edwin; The National Portrait Gallery.*
William Samuel Johnson — *John Wesley Jarvis; The National Portrait Gallery.*
Richard Basset — *Unknown; Delaware State Museums.*
George Read — *Robert Edge Pine; The National Portrait Gallery.*
William Few — *Bowen;* Park Avenue Photo, Rochester.*
Charles Carroll off Carollton — *Albert Newsam; The National Portrait Gallery.*
Tristam Dalton — *John Trumbull; Yale University Art Gallery.*
Caleb Strong — *Tappan Bradford; The National Portrait Gallery.*
John Langdon — *Max Rosenthal; The National Portrait Gallery.*
William Paterson — *Bowen;* Park Avenue Photo; Rochester.*
Philemon Dickinson — *Bowen;* Park Avenue Photo; Rochester.*
Rufus King — *Gilbert Stuart; The National Portrait Gallery.*
Philip Schuyler — *Unknown; The Bronx County Historical Society.*
Benjamin Hawkins — *Bowen;* Park Avenue Photo; Rochester.*
Samuel Johnston — *Bowen;* Park Avenue Photo; Rochester.*
William Maclay — *Unknown; Public Domain.*
Robert Morris — *Robert Edge Pine; The National Portrait Gallery.*
Theodore Foster — *Bowen;* Park Avenue Photo, Rochester.*
Pierce Butler — *Bowen;* Park Avenue Photo, Rochester.*
Ralph Izard — *John Trumbull; Yale University Art Gallery.*
William Grayson — *Unknown; University of Virginia Library.*
James Monroe — *James Herring; The National Portrait Gallery.*
Richard Henry Lee — *Charles William Peale; The National Portrait Gallery.*

---

*Copied from Bowen, "The Centennial of Washington's First Inaugural".

ABOUT THE AUTHOR

RICHARD W. STREB born in Rochester, NY, served three years in the U. S. Navy aboard the aircraft carrier USS ESSEX where he earned 13 battle stars, the American theater and the Asiatic/Pacific ribbons, the Philippine Liberation Medal and the Presidential Citation from Harry S Truman.

He received his B.A. from Syracuse University and his MA and Ed.D from Columbia University. His doctoral dissertation won the Exemplary Dissertation Award from the National Council for the Social Studies for excellence in research, for the quality of the writing and for contribution to our understanding of the Social Studies. He taught at all levels of the educational system from elementary school through the graduate level for 32 years. Doctor Streb retired from Teachers College, Columbia University In the fall of 1989.

He and his wife Rosemary live in Roanoke Virginia.

INDEX

Ableman v. *Booth* (1859), **5**:30
Act Concerning the District of Columbia (1801), **5**:90
Adams, Abigail Smith, **1**:13
Adams, John, **1**:12-13, 15, 51, 85, 100, 118, 122, 125; **3**:7, 12, 59, 99, 133; **4**:14, 140; **6**:9, 14
  death, **1**:85; **6**:9
  observations, **1**:11, 19, 88; **3**:94; **4**:28, 53; **5**:12, 17
  presidency, **2**:63, 68; **3**:35, 60; **4**:89; **5**:10, 93, 98; **6**:6-7, 89, 97, 98
Adams, John Quincy, **3**:77; **6**:2, 14-15, 90, 98
Adams, Samuel, **1**:3, 10-11, 16, 118, 122; **2**:12; **4**:50
Adamson Act, **5**:49
"Affair of Fort Wilson," **1**:63
Agnew, Spiro, **6**:77
Agricultural Adjustment Act, **5**:63
"Alabama claims," **5**:38
Alamance, Battle of (1771), **2**:100

Alaska, **6**:37, 51
Albany Congress (1754), **1**:18
Albany Plan of Union (1754), **2**:39; **3**:1, 132
"Albany Regency," **6**:19
Alexander, Robert, **1**:123
Algeciras Conference, **6**:53
Alsop, John, **1**:122, 123
American Colonization Society, **6**:13
American Communications Association v. *Douds* (1950), **5**:67
American Independent Party, **6**:101
American Party (Know-Nothing Party), **6**:29, 99
American Relief Committee, **6**:63
American Revolution. *See* Revolutionary War
Ames, Fisher, **2**:21; **4**:12, 14, 17, 20, 50-51, 133, 137
Anderson, John B., **6**:102
Andre, John, **4**:79

141

Annapolis Convention, **2**:ix, 62, 79
Antifederalists, **3**:11, 18, 20, 123; **4**:3-4, 5-6, 7, 13, 17, 141, 143
Anti-Masonic Party, **6**:90, 98
Arkansas, **6**:84, 85
Armstrong Insurance Commission, **5**:58
Arthur, Chester Alan, **6**:44-45, 54, 96
Articles of Confederation, **2**:ix, 30, 51, 72, 73; **3**:2, 10, 132; **4**:1-2; **5**:1; **6**:86
Ashe, John Baptista, **4**:84
"Association Test," **3**:61
Assumption issue (state debts), **4**:135, 137, 138

Bailey v. *Drexel Furniture* (1922), **5**:54
Baker v. *Carr* (1962), **5**:72
Baldwin, Abraham, **2**:102-103, 108, 109; **4**:38
Baldwin, Henry, **5**:84
Bank of the United States, **4**:36, 46, 55, 87, 88, 119, 125, 139-140; **5**:24, 28; **6**:17, 23
Barbour, Philip P., **5**:85
Barlow, Joel, **2**:103
Barlow, Ruth, **2**:102-103
Barron v. *Baltimore* (1833), **5**:24-25
Bartlett, Josiah, **1**:4-5, 118, 122
Bassett, Richard, **2**:62-63; **3**:13, 34-35, 126, 130
Beckley, John, **4**:13
Bedford, Gunning, Jr., **2**:57, 58-59, 109; **4**:36
Bell, Alexander Graham, **5**:40

Bell, John, **6**:99
Benson, A. L., **6**:100
Benson, Egbert, **4**:22, 74-75
Bentsen, Lloyd, **6**:91
Berlin Blockade, **6**:67
Bidwell, John, **6**:100
Bill of Rights
  First House and, **4**:11-23
  parchment copies, **4**:145
  ratification, **3**:129; **4**:141, 143-147
  Senate role, **3**:120, 127-129
Bill of Rights Day, **4**:145
Birney, James G., **6**:99
Black, Hugo L., **5**:64, 87
"Blackguard Charlie" (Charles Pinckney nickname), **2**:95
Black Hawk War, **6**:26
Blackmun, Harry A., **5**:88
Blaine, James G., **6**:43, 49, 99
Blair, John, **2**:76-77; **5**:84
Bland, Theodoric, **4**:16, 116
Blatchford, Samuel, **5**:86
"Bleeding Kansas," **6**:31
Bloodworth, Timothy, **4**:85
Blount, William, **2**:48-49, 82-83
Booth, John Wilkes, **6**:35
Boston Massacre (1770), **1**:11
Boudinot, Elias, **4**:12, 68-69, 131; **6**:87
Bourn, Benjamin, **4**:104
Bowdoin, James, **2**:ix
Bowen, Catherine Drinker, **2**:x
Boxer Rebellion, **6**:63
Bradley, Joseph P., **5**:85
Brandeis, Louis D., **5**:53, 86
Braxton, Carter, **1**:xi, 86, 92-93, 118, 122
Brearley, David, **2**:30-31, 57; **6**:2, 88
Breckinridge, John C., **6**:99
Brennan, William J., Jr., **5**:88

Brewer, David J., **5:**86
Breyer, Stephen, **5:**88
Broom, Jacob, **2:**64-65
Brown, Henry B., **5:**86
Brown, John, **4:**117
Brownell, Herbert, **5:**76
Brown University, **3:**98
Brown v. Board of Education of Topeka (1954), **5:**71, 80
Bryan, William Jennings, **6:**51, 100
Buchanan, James, **6:**2, 32-33, 39, 99
Buena Vista, Battle of (1847), **6:**27
Buffon, Georges, **1:**85
Bull Moose Party. *See* Progressive Party
Bullock, Archibald, **1:**124
Burger, Warren Earl, **5:**8-9, 73, 74-78, 88, 99
Burke, Aedanus, **4:**21, 22, 106-107, 136
Burr, Aaron, **2:**25, 34; **3:**99; **5:**24; **6:**9, 89, 98
Burton, Harold H., **5:**87
Bush, George Herbert Walker, **6:**82-83, 102
Bush, Prescott, **6:**82
Butler, Benjamin F., **6:**99
Butler, Pierce (1744-1822), **2:**96-97; **3:**13, 104-106, 124, 126, 131; **5:**87
Butler, Pierce (1810-1867), **2:**97
Byrnes, James F., **5:**87

Cadwalader, Lambert, **4:**70
Calder v. Bull (1798), **5:**18
Calhoun, John Caldwell, **3:**xi; **6:**17, 25

California, **6:**27, 29, 74
Camillus (pseudonym), **4:**50
Campbell, John A., **5:**85
Canada, **5:**8; **6:**23, 25
Capitol building (Washington, D.C), **3:**15-16, 76, 134; **5:**98-99
Cardozo, Benjamin N., **5:**57, 63, 87
Carroll, Charles, **1:**ix, 73, 78-79, 118, 124; **2:**72; **3:**13, 46-47, 126, 129, 130
Carroll, Daniel, **1:**ix; **2:**72-73; **4:**42, 43, 138, 139
Carroll, John, **2:**72; **4:**43
Carter, Jimmy, **6:**78-79, 102
Cass, Lewis, **6:**99
Caswell, Richard, **1:**124
Catron, John, **5:**85
Census, **4:**136
Central Intelligence Agency, **6:**83
Chafin, Eugene W., **6:**100
Channing, William Ellery, **1:**21
Chase, Salmon Portland, **5:**31-35, 85
Chase, Samuel, **1:**72-73, 74, 79, 118, 124; **2:**34, 102; **5:**17, 84
Cheney, Charles, **5:**42
Cherokee Indians, **4:**88, 93
Chew, Benjamin, **1:**62
Chickasaw Indians, **4:**88
Chief justices
  biographies, **5:**7-83
  longevity record, **5:**21
  only former president as, **6:**55
China, **6:**51, 62-63
Chisholm v. Georgia (1793), **2:**48, 77; **5:**9
Christensen, P. P., **6:**100
Civil Rights Acts, **6:**73

Civil Rights Cases (1883), **5**:40
Civil service, **6**:45, 47, 49, 53
Civil War, **5**:30, 32, 33; **6**:35, 39, 42-43, 47, 49, 50
Clark, Abraham, **1**:ix, 46-47, 118, 122
Clark, Ed, **6**:102
Clark, Tom C., **5**:87
Clarke, John H., **5**:87
Clay, Henry, **1**:80; **3**:xi, 77; **6**:11, 15, 21, 23, 25, 29, 98, 99
Cleveland, Frances, **6**:47
Cleveland, Grover, **5**:42, 43, 47-48; **6**:46-47, 49, 91, 99, 100
Clifford, Nathan, **5**:85
Clinton, DeWitt, **6**:98
Clinton, George, **1**:122, 123; **2**:24; **4**:6, 15, 74, 78, 81, 82; **6**:98
Clinton, William Jefferson, **6**:84-85, 102
Clymer, George, **1**:viii, 56-57, 118, 125; **2**:44-45, 46, 108; **4**:92-93
Coercive Acts (1774), **1**:122, 126; **3**:112
Coles, Isaac, **4**:118
Columbia University, **2**:18; **3**:29-30, 31, 32, 77
Commerce clause, **5**:24
Compromise of 1850, **6**:29, 31
Confederate States of America, **6**:23
Confederation Congress, **2**:40; **3**:2, 10, 72, 75, 83, 86, 108, 115, 117, 120; **4**:1, 4, 7
Congress
  Confederation (*see* Confederation Congress)
  Continental (*see* Continental Congress)
  first (*see* First Congress; First House of Representatives; First Senate)
  powers granted to, **3**:7-9
  salaries, **4**:144
  Supreme Court and, **5**:89-92, 93-96
  use of term, **3**:3
  See also House of Representatives; Senate
Congressional immunity, **3**:6
Congressional Record, **3**:5, 21; **4**:13
Conkling, Roscoe, **6**:43, 45
Connecticut, **1**:22-23, 24-25, 26-27, 28-29, 122; **2**:18-19, 20-21, 104, 111; **3**:26-28, 29-32, 130; **4**:8, 26, 27-28, 29, 30-31, 32-33; **5**:16
Connecticut Compromise, **1**:23; **2**:21, 30, 32, 57; **4**:38
Considerations on the Nature and Extent of the Legislative Authority of the British Parliament (Wilson), **2**:48
Constitution
  amendments (*see* specific amendment numbers)
  Bill of Rights (*see* Bill of Rights)
  biographies of signers, **2**:2-103
  creation of judiciary, **5**:1-3
  enduring nature, **4**:1
  interpreting, **3**:20-21 (*see also* Judicial review)
  list of signers, **2**:110; **3**:126
  ratification, **1**:5; **2**:111; **3**:130-131; **4**:3-4
  revenue measures, **4**:131
Constitutional Convention (1787), **3**:132; **4**:2-4, 124; **5**:89-90; **6**:86, 88

committee membership,
  2:108-109
delegates, **1**:23, 53, 63; **2**:ix-x,
  2.2-105; **3**:20, 27, 31, 38, 41,
  55, 59, 67, 75, 105, 123;
  4:28, 42, 123; **5**:1-2, 13, 17;
  6:4-5, 10
  nonsigning delegates, **2**:104-
    107
  presidency issues, **6**:1-2
  president of, **2**:2-3
Constitutional Union Party,
  6:99
Contee, Benjamin, **4**:44
Continental Army, **2**:24, 40, 45,
  46; **4**:32; **6**:6
Continental Congresses, **3**:1-2,
  132
  delegates, **2**:50-51, 60-61;
    3:37, 59, 72, 79, 94, 120,
    123, 126; **5**:7
  presidency, **1**:3; **6**:86
  in 1776, **1**:122-126
Conway Cabal, **2**:40
Coolidge, Calvin, **5**:62; **6**:60-61,
  96, 101
Copyright, **4**:136
Countryman Letters, **4**:28
"Court Packing" plan, **5**:60
Cox, James N., **6**:100
Crawford, William H., **6**:98
Creek Indians, **3**:42, 83-84, 123
Cresap, Michael, **2**:105
Crittenden, John, **6**:37
Cuba, **6**:33, 51, 71
Curtis, Benjamin R., **5**:85
Cushing, William, **5**:16, 22, 84
Czolgosz, Leon, **6**:51

Dalton, Tristram, **3**:13, 52-53,
  92, 126, 130

Dana, Richard Henry, **1**:21
Daniel, Peter V., **5**:85
Daugherty, Henry, **6**:59
Davie, William Richardson,
  2:106-107, 109
Davis, David, **5**:85
Davis, Jefferson, **6**:31
Davis, John W., **6**:101
Day, William R., **5**:86
Dayton, Elias, **2**:34
Dayton, Jonathan, **2**:34-35
Debs, Eugene V., **6**:100
Debs case, **5**:44, 48
Declaration of Independence,
  3:61; **4**:1
  biographies of signers, **1**:2-
    113
  non-signing members of
    Congress, **1**:123-124
  order of signing, **1**:3
  physician signatories, **1**:4
  preliminaries to, **1**:126-27
  signers, **1**:118-21; **3**:37, 47,
    120, 123, 126; **4**:27-28
  text, **1**:114-17
Declaration of Rights (Virginia), **4**:19, 143-144, 145
*Defense of the Constitutions of
  the United States of America* (Adams), **6**:7
De Lancey family, **2**:28-29;
  3:107, 108
Delaware, **1**:66-67, 68-69, 70-71,
  122; **2**:56-57, 58-59, 60-61,
  62-63, 64-65, 111; **3**:34-35,
  36-38, 130; **4**:4-5, 8, 36, 144
Delian League, **3**:1
Democratic Party, **5**:27, 28;
  6:19, 21, 25, 30, 33, 35, 37,
  57, 67, 71, 73, 79, 85, 90,
  91, 98, 99, 100, 101, 102
Democratic-Republican Party,

2:79; **3**:19; **4**:124; **5**:90, 91, 92; **6**:9, 11, 17, 89, 97, 98
Denby, Edwin, **6**:59
Dennis v. *United States* (1951), **5**:67-68
Dewey, George, **6**:53
Dewey, Thomas E., **6**:101
Dickinson, John, **1**:viii, 122, 123; **2**:60-61, 108; **3**:69
Dickinson, Philemon, **3**:69-70, 124, 126, 130
Dickinson, Samuel, **3**:69
District of Columbia. *See* Washington, D.C.
Dixiecrats. *See* States' Rights Party
Dobbs, Arthur, **2**:83
Douglas, Stephen A., **6**:31, 35, 99
Douglas, William O., **5**:63, 78, 87
Dred Scott v. *Sandford* (1857), **5**:29-30
Duane, James, **1**:123
Due process, **5**:39, 43-44, 76
Dukakis, Michael S., **6**:102
Du Pont, E. I., **2**:65
Duvall, Gabriel, **5**:84

E.C. Knight case (1895), **5**:44, 48
Eisenhower, Dwight David, **5**:70, 75; **6**:68-69, 75, 101
Elastic clause, **5**:24
Elections, presidential. *See* Presidential elections
Electoral College, **6**:7, 9, 15, 16, 41, 49, 88-93
Eleventh Amendment, **2**:48, 77; **4**:40; **5**:9, 18
Ellery, William, **1**:20-21, 118, 122

Ellsworth, Oliver, **2**:77, 90, 104, 109; **3**:13, 26-28, 123, 126, 129, 130; **4**:133; **5**:3, 15-19, 22, 84, 90, 92
Elmer, Jonathan, **3**:13, 71-72, 124, 126, 130
Emancipation Proclamation, **6**:35
Embargo Act (1807), **2**:7; **4**:31
England. *See* Great Britain
"Era of Good Feelings" (Monroe presidency), **6**:12
Erie Canal, **2**:53
Essex Junto, **3**:62
Etowah Campaign, **4**:87
European Food Program, **6**:63

Fall, Albert B., **6**:59
Farmer-Labor Party, **6**:100
Faubus, Orval, **5**:71
Federal Hall (New York City), **3**:15, 133, 134; **4**:12, 15; **6**:5
Federalist, The, **2**:25, 79; **4**:4, 6, 123; **5**:3, 4, 8, 89; **6**:10-11
Federalists, **2**:14; **3**:18, 19, 21, 55, 62, 76, 83, 123, 126, 128; **4**:3-4, 5, 6-7, 11, 19, 135; **5**:22, 23, 90, 91, 92; **6**:7, 13, 89, 97, 98
Federal Reserve System, **6**:57
Federal Trade Commission, **6**:57
Few, James, **2**:100
Few, William, **2**:93, 100-101; **3**:13, 40-42, 124, 126, 130
Field, Stephen J., **5**:35, 39, 85
Fifteenth Amendment, **5**:40
Fillmore, Millard, **6**:28-29, 96, 99
First Amendment, **3**:6; **4**:144-145; **5**:72, 82

First Congress
  accomplishments, **4:**131-142
  first meeting, **4:**11-12
  See also First House of Representatives; First Senate
First House of Representatives
  accomplishments, **4:**131-142
  Bill of Rights role, **4:**11-23
  Clerk, **4:**13
  delegates, **4:**25-130
  election, **4:**7-10
  organization, **4:**13-14
  procedures, **4:**17
  quorum, **3:**11, 133
  records, **4:**13
  revenue measures, **4:**14-15, 131-132, 139
  size, **4:**13
  Speaker, **4:**12-13
First Senate
  Bill of Rights role, **3:**127-129; **4:**22-23
  election for, **3:**10-11
  issues, **3:**17-22
  Judicial Branch creation, **4:**133
  meeting dates, **3:**12
  meeting locations, **3:**14-16
  organization, **4:**14
  in profile, **3:**123-126
  salary, **3:**5-6
  term expirations, **3:**4, 13, 133
Fisk, Clinton B., **6:**100
Fitzsimmons, Thomas, **2:**46-47; **4:**94
Flagburning, **5:**82
Florida, **6:**15, 41
Floyd, John, **6:**98
Floyd, Kitty, **1:**31
Floyd, William, **1:**30-31, 118, 122; **4:**76-77

Ford, Gerald Rudolph, **6:**76-77, 79, 83, 96, 102
Fortas, Abe, **5:**73, 88
Foster, Abel, **4:**62
Foster, Dwight, **3:**99
Foster, Theodore, **3:**98-100, 124, 126, 131
Fourteen Points, **6:**57
Fourteenth Amendment, **5:**35, 38-39, 40, 44, 76
France, **2:**52, 93; **3:**15, 17, 47, 60
Frankfurter, Felix, **5:**59, 87
Franklin, Benjamin, **1:**viii, xi-xii, 12, 42, 52-53, 54, 79, 118, 122, 125; **2:**28, 38-39, 87, 109; **3:**47, 108; **4:**133-134, 136, 142
Franklin, State of, **4:**86
Franklin, William, **1:**xi-xii, 45; **2:**39
Freeman, Elizabeth, **4:**58
Free Soil Party, **5:**33; **6:**19, 99
Fremont, John C., **6:**99
Fuller, Melville Weston, **5:**41-45, 86
Funding and Assumption Act, **4:**138

Gadsden Purchase, **6:**31
Gage, Thomas, **1:**122; **3:**30
Gale, George, **4:**45, 138
Gallatin, Albert, **3:**76
"Gamecock" (Thomas Sumter's nickname), **4:**111
Garfield, James Abram, **6:**42-43, 95, 99
Gaspeé (British ship), **1:**18-19
Gates, Horatio, **2:**40
Gazette of the United States, **4:**13

Genêt, "Citizen" Edmond, **2**:52
Georgia, **1**:108-109, 110-111, 112-113, 122, 123; **2**:100-101, 102-103, 107, 111; **3**:40-42, 43-44, 130; **4**:5, 38, 39-40; **6**:78, 79
Gerry, Elbridge, **1**:viii, 16-17, 87, 118, 122, 124; **2**:104, 109; **3**:127; **4**:22, 52-53, 118
Gerrymander, **4**:53
Gilbert, Cass, **5**:99
Giles, William Branch, **4**:116, 119
Gilman, John Taylor, **2**:9
Gilman, Nicholas, **2**:6, 8-9; **4**:63
Ginsberg, Ruth Bader, **5**:88
Gitlow v. *New York* (1925), **5**:54
Glass v. *The Sloop Betsey* (1794), **5**:9-10
Goldberg, Arthur J., **5**:88
Goodhue, Benjamin, **4**:54
"Good Neighbor Policy," **6**:65
Gorham, Nathaniel, **2**:12-13, 62, 108, 109; **6**:87
"Grand Convention." *See* Constitutional Convention (1787)
Grant, Ulysses Simpson, **5**:34, 38, 95; **6**:3, 38-39, 54, 99
Gray, Horace, **5**:86
Grayson, William, **3**:13, 112-113, 117, 123, 124, 126, 128, 131
Great Britain, **3**:2, 3, 17-18
Great Compromise, **2**:18, 87, 90, 102; **3**:2-3; **5**:2, 13, 17
Great Depression, **5**:59; **6**:62, 63, 64, 65
Great Society (LBJ program), **6**:73

Greeley, Horace, **6**:99
Greenback-Labor Party, **6**:99
Greene, Nathanael, **1**:37; **2**:90; **3**:108
Gregg v. *Georgia* (1976), **5**:77
Grier, Robert C., **5**:85
Griffin, Cyrus, **6**:87
Griffin, Samuel, **4**:120
Grout, Jonathan, **4**:55
Guiteau, Charles, **6**:43
Gunn, James, **3**:13, 42, 43-44, 126, 130
Gwinnett, Button, **1**:108-109, 113, 118, 122

Hale, John P., **6**:99
"Half-Breeds" (Republican Party faction), **6**:43, 45
Halifax Resolves, **1**:127
Hall, Lyman, **1**:109, 110-111, 113, 119, 122
Hamilton, Alexander, **1**:37; **2**:24-25, 29, 42, 62, 108, 109; **3**:14, 17, 21-22, 75, 79-80; **4**:79, 106, 124, 137-138, 143, 147; **5**:3, 8
  opponents, **2**:79, 102; **6**:9
  supporters, **2**:46, 68; **3**:76, 105; **6**:10
  Treasury secretary, **3**:95; **4**:20, 109, 132-133, 134-135, 139, 140-141
  views, **3**:18, 19-21; **4**:2-3, 4, 5, 6, 18; **5**:89
Hancock, John, **1**:2-3, 16-17, 119, 122; **2**:12; **6**:86, 87
Hancock, Winfield S., **6**:99
Hand, Learned, **5**:57
Hankey, J. Frank, **6**:100
Hanna, Mark, **6**:51
Hanson, John, **6**:87

Harding, Warren Gamaliel, **5:**48, 53; **6:**3, 55, 58-59, 61, 63, 95, 100
Harlan, John Marshall, **5:**85, 88
Harrison, Benjamin (?1726-1791), **1:**xi, 86, 92, 119, 122; **6:**21
Harrison, Benjamin (1833-1901), **6:**48-49, 55, 91, 100
Harrison, John Scott, **6:**48
Harrison, William Henry, **6:**20-21, 23, 48, 95, 98
Hart, John, **1:**44-45, 119, 122
Hartford Convention, **2:**53
Hartley, Thomas, **4:**95
Hathorn, John, **4:**78
Hawaii, **6:**51
Hawkins, Benjamin, **3:**82-84, 123, 126, 131
Hayes, Rutherford Birchard, **6:**40-41, 45, 99
Haynes, George H., **3:**21
Henry, John, **3:**13, 48-49, 126, 130
Henry, Patrick, **1:**11, 83; **3:**115, 117; **4:**5, 6, 8-9, 118, 123, 128, 146, 147
Hermitage (Andrew Jackson's home), **6:**17
Hewes, Joseph, **1:**xi, 96-97, 119, 122
Heyward, Thomas, Jr., **1:**xi, 102-103, 119, 122
Hiester, Daniel, **4:**96
Hill, David, **5:**47-48
"His Rotundity" (John Adams's nickname), **3:**108
Hiss, Alger, **6:**75
Holmes, Oliver Wendell, Jr., **5:**43, 44, 49, 63, 86
Homestead Bill (1846), **6:**37
Hooper, William, **1:**94-95, 119, 124

Hoover, Herbert Clark, **5:**58, 63; **6:**2, 59, 62-63, 101
Hoover, J. Edgar, **5:**62
Hopkins, Samuel, **4:**136
Hopkins, Stephen, **1:**18-19, 119, 122; **3:**99
Hopkinson, Francis, **1:**42-43, 119, 122
Hosmer, Titus, **1:**123
Hospers, John, **6:**91
House of Representatives, **3:**4-5, 6, 7, 7-8; **6:**89, 90, 92
  Bill of Rights, **3:**128-129
  first (*see* First House of Representatives)
  Speaker (*see* Speaker of the House)
House Un-American Activities Committee, **6:**75
Houston, William Churchill (New Jersey), **2:**105
Houstoun, William (Georgia), **2:**107
Howe, William, **3:**113
Huger, Daniel, **4:**108
Hughes, Charles Evans, **5:**30, 56-60, 86, 87, 95; **6:**59, 100
Humphrey, Hubert H., **6:**101
Humphreys, Charles, **1:**122, 123
Hunt, Ward, **5:**85
Huntington, Benjamin, **1:**27; **4:**26
Huntington, Samuel, **1:**24-25, 29, 112, 119, 122; **6:**87
Hustler v. *Falwell* (1988), **5:**82
Hylton v. *United States* (1796), **5:**90

Illinois, **6:**34, 81
Impeachment, **2:**34, 82; **3:**7; **5:**34; **6:**37, 75, 95

Inauguration, presidential
  date, **6:**94-95
  first, **4:**15-16
Independent Party, **6:**102
Indiana, **6:**48-49
Indians. *See* Native Americans
Ingersoll, Jared, **2:**48-49, 77, 83
INS v. *Chadha* (1983), **5:**77
Intolerable Acts. *See* Coercive
  Acts
Iowa, **6:**62
Iran, **6:**79
Iredell, James, **1:**63; **5:**84
Iroquois Confederacy, **3:**1
Izard, Ralph, **3:**13, 107-109,
  124, 126, 128, 131

Jackson, Andrew, **5:**24, 27-28,
  94; **6:**2, 11, 13, 15, 16-17,
  19, 33, 90, 98
Jackson, Howell E., **5:**86
Jackson, James, **4:**19, 39,
  137
Jackson, Robert H., **5:**59, 64,
  66, 80, 87
Jameson, J. Franklin, **3:**21
Janes and Beebe Ironworks
  (New York City), **3:**16, 134
Japan, **6:**29, 67
Jay, John, **1:**123; **3:**18, 55, 117;
  4:4, 6, 133; **5:**3, 7-10, 22, 84,
  97, 98; **6:**10, 87, 98
Jay's Treaty, **2:**90, 94, 102;
  3:18, 28, 59, 76, 99; **4:**50-51,
  98, 119; **5:**14
Jefferson, Thomas, **1:**13, 43,
  80, 81, 84-85, 89, 119, 122,
  125; **2:**105; **3:**99, 129, 132;
  4:1, 4, 19, 50, 133, 137-138,
  145; **6:**8-9, 12, 97
  presidency, **2:**7, 94; **3:**60;
  4:63, 89, 113; **5:**91, 94; **6:**2,
  11, 13, 89, 95, 98
  supporters, **2:**79, 102; **3:**17,
  19, 20, 76, 117; **4:**123, 126,
  127; **6:**7, 15
  views, **1:**22, 51; **2:**21, 25;
  3:14, 18-19
Jenifer, Daniel of St. Thomas,
  2:28, 70-71
Johnson, Andrew, **5:**34, 94;
  6:36-37, 39, 95, 96
Johnson, Lyndon Baines, **5:**73;
  6:2, 72-73, 81, 96, 101
Johnson, Samuel, **3:**30
Johnson, Thomas, **1:**123; **5:**84
Johnson, William (Supreme
  Court justice), **5:**84
Johnson, William Samuel (Connecticut senator), **2:**18-19,
  108, 109; **3:**13, 29-32, 124,
  126, 130
Johnston, Samuel, **3:**85-87,
  123, 126, 131
Jones, Joseph, **3:**116
Jones, Willie, **2:**87
*Journal of a Residence in
  America* (Kemble), **2:**97
Judicial review, **5:**2-3, 23, 89-92
Judiciary Act of 1789, **3:**32, 55,
  105; **4:**59, 62, 133; **5:**3, 4, 9,
  17
Judiciary Act of 1801, **5:**90, 93
Judiciary Act of 1869, **5:**95

Kansas, **6:**31, 33, 68
Kansas-Nebraska Act (1854),
  6:31
Kennedy, Anthony M., **5:**88
Kennedy, John Fitzgerald, **3:**xi;
  5:73; **6:**70-71, 73, 84, 95,
  101

Kennedy, Joseph P., **6:**70, 71
Kentucky, **4:**117; **6:**26, 34
Key, Francis Scott, **2:**69
King, John Alsop, **2:**15
King, Rufus, **2:**14-15, 58, 93, 108, 109; **3:**74-77, 126, 131; **6:**98
Kissam, Benjamin, **5:**7
Kitchen Cabinet, **6:**16
Kleberg, Richard M., **6:**72
Know-Nothing Party. *See* American Party
Knox, Henry, **4:**135
Kossuth, Louis, **6:**29
Kuwait, **6:**83

Lafayette, Marquis de, **2:**35; **4:**3
La Follette, Robert M., Sr., **3:**xi; **6:**101
Laissez faire philosophy, **5:**39-40, 42, 43, 47
Lamar, Joseph R., **5:**86
Lamar, Lucius Q., **5:**86
Landon, Alfred M., **6:**101
Langdon, John, **2:**6-7, 108; **3:**12, 13, 58-60, 124, 126, 128, 131, 133; **4:**14
Lansing, John, Jr., **2:**24, 104-105
Latrobe, Benjamin, **5:**98
Laurance, John, **4:**79-80, 132
Laurens, Henry, **6:**86
Lawson, Peter, **2:**62; **3:**34
League of Nations, **6:**57, 59
Lecompton Constitution, **6:**33
Lee, Francis Lightfoot, **1:**90-91, 119, 122
Lee, "Lighthorse Harry," **4:**121
Lee, Richard Bland, **4:**21, 121-122, 138, 139

Lee, Richard Henry, **1:**ix, 63, 82-83, 90, 91, 119, 124, 127; **3:**11, 13, 90, 119-121, 123, 124, 126, 127, 128, 131, 132; **4:**23; **6:**87
Lee, Robert E., **1:**90; **6:**39
Lee, William, **1:**91
Legal Tender Cases (1870), **5:**35
Legislative veto, **5:**77
Lemke, William, **6:**101
L'Enfant, Pierre Charles, **3:**15; **4:**12, 43; **5:**98
Leonard, George, **4:**56
Letters from a Pennsylvania Farmer (Dickinson), **2:**60; **3:**69
Letters of a Landholder (Ellsworth), **3:**27-28
Lewis, Francis, **1:**34-35, 119, 122
Lewis, Mrs. Francis, **1:**35
Lewis and Clark Expedition, **6:**9
Liberia, **6:**13
Libertarian Party, **6:**102
Liberty Bell, **5:**25
Liberty Party, **5:**33; **6:**25, 99
Lincoln, Abraham, **5:**30, 32, 33, 94; **6:**3, 34-35, 37, 39, 95, 99
Lincoln, Benjamin, **2:**94
Livermore, Samuel, **4:**64, 65
Livingston, H. Brockholst, **5:**84
Livingston, Philip, **1:**ix, **1:**xi, 32-33, 119, 122
Livingston, Robert R., **1:**122, 123, 125
Livingston, William, **1:**ix; **2:**28-29, 45, 108; **3:**68, 70
Lloyd, Thomas, **4:**13
Lochner v. *New York* (1905), **5:**43-44, 48

Locke, John, **3:**2; **6:**1
Logan (Indian chief), **2:**105
Long's Tavern (Washington, D.C.), **5:**98
Louisiana, **6:**41
Louisiana Purchase (1803), **2:**34; **6:**9
Lurton, Horace H., **5:**86
Lynch, Thomas, Jr., **1:**104-105, 119, 122
Lynch, Thomas, Sr., **1:**105, 122, 124
Lyon, Matthew, **2:**33

MacArthur, Douglas, **6:**68
McKinley Tariff (1890), **6:**51
Maclay, William, **3:**13, 21-22, 32, 42, 47, 49, 53, 67, 70, 80, 83, 90-92, 95, 101, 106, 120, 123, 124, 126, 128, 130; **4:**15, 93, 102, 137
Madison, Dolley Payne, **1:**31; **2:**79; **6:**11
Madison, James, **1:**31; **4:**36; **5:**3
  Bill of Rights role, **4:**8-10, 17-23, 143, 144, 146
  Constitution, 278-79; **2:**51, 108, 109; **4:**2, 4, 5, 6, 7
  in First House, **3:**117, 128; **4:**12, 13, 14, 16, 123-124, 130, 132, 133, 135, 137, 138, 139-140
  presidency, **2:**7, 93; **3:**60; **5:**91; **6:**10-11, 13, 15, 98
Maine, **4:**61
Maine, USS (ship), **6:**51
Mangum, W. P., **6:**98
Marbury, William, **5:**91
Marbury v. *Madison* (1803), **5:**23, 90-92
Marcy, William, **6:**19

Marion, Francis, **2:**90
Marshall, John, **1:**17, 80; **4:**5; **5:**20-25, 84, 90-92; **6:**7
Marshall, Thurgood, **5:**88
Marshall Plan, **6:**67
Martin, Alexander, **2:**106
Martin, Luther, **2:**70-71, 105, 108, 109
Maryland, **1:**72-73, 74-75, 76-77, 78-79, 122, 123, 126; **2:**68-69, 70-71, 72-73, 105, 111; **3:**48-49, 130; **4:**4-5, 42-43, 44-45, 46, 47, 48, 138, 144
Mason, George, **2:**106, 109; **3:**127; **4:**3, 5, 19, 145
Mason, Jeremiah, **3:**74
Massachusetts, **1:**2-3, 10-11, 12-13, 14-15, 16-17, 122, 126; **2:**12-13, 14-15, 104, 111; **3:**52-53, 54-56, 130; **4:**4-5, 50-51, 52-53, 54, 55, 56, 57, 58-59, 60-61, 137, 138; **6:**6, 14, 60-61, 71
"Massachusetts formula," **4:**4
Mathews, George, **4:**40
Matthews, Stanley, **5:**85
McClellan, George B., **6:**99
McClurg, James, **2:**106
McCulloch v. *Maryland* (1819), **5:**24
McGovern, George S., **6:**85, 102
McHenry, James, **2:**68-69
McIntosh, George, **1:**109
McIntosh, Lachlan, **1:**109
McIntosh, William, **3:**84
McKean, Thomas, **1:**67, 68, 70-71, 119, 122, 124; **6:**87
McKenna, Joseph, **5:**86
McKinley, John, **5:**85
McKinley, William, **5:**52; **6:**50-51, 53, 95, 100

McKinly, John, **1:**69
McLaurin v. Oklahoma State Regents (1950), **5:**68
McLean, John, **5:**84
McReynolds, James C., **5:**62, 86
Meade, George, **2:**46
Mecklenburg Resolutions, **1:**127
Meigs, Josiah, **4:**38
Mellon, Andrew W., **6:**59
Melville, Herman, **6:**45
Mercer, John Francis, **2:**105
Mexican Revolution, **6:**57
Mexican War, **6:**25, 27, 31, 35
Michigan, **6:**76
Middleton, Arthur, **1:**xi, 103, 106-107, 119, 122; **2:**92
Middleton, Henry, **1:**124; **6:**86
"Midnight judges," **2:**63; **3:**35; **4:**75
Mifflin, Thomas, **1:**123; **2:**40-41, 46; **6:**87
Military-industrial complex, **6:**69
Miller, Samuel F., **5:**35, 85
Minton, Sherman, **5:**87
Miracle at Philadelphia (Bowen), **2:**x
Missouri, **6:**66, 67
Missouri Compromise (1820), **2:**15, 95; **4:**60; **5:**29; **6:**13
Mondale, Walter F., **6:**102
Monmouth, Battle of (1778), **3:**70
Monroe, James, **1:**80; **2:**14; **3:**76, 116-118, 123, 126, 131; **4:**9, 40; **6:**12-13, 98
Monroe Doctrine, **6:**13, 15
Montesquieu, Baron Charles de, **3:**2; **4:**2
Moody, William H., **5:**86

Moore, Alfred, **5:**84
Moore, Andrew, **4:**125
Morocco, **6:**53
Morris, Gouverneur, **1:**ix, 37; **2:**18, 52-53, 109; **3:**117; **4:**20; **6:**88, 92
Morris, Lewis, **1:**ix, 36-37, 120, 124
Morris, Robert, **1:**viii, xi, 48-49, 89, 120, 122; **2:**12, 42-43, 61; **3:**13, 14, 93-95, 123, 124, 126, 128, 130; **4:**16
Morton, John, **1:**54-55, 63, 120, 122
Muhlenberg, Frederick Augustus Conrad, **4:**12-13, 14, 97, 98, 141, 145
Muhlenberg, John Peter Gabriel, **4:**99
Muller v. Oregon (1908), **5:**44, 48
Munn v. Illinois (1877), **5:**39
Murphy, Frank, **5:**87
"My Days Have Been So Wondrous Free" (song), **1:**43
Myers v. United States (1926), **5:**54

Nationalist Republican Party, **6:**98
National League of Cities v. Usery (1976), **5:**81
National Republican Party, **6:**90, 97
Native Americans, **3:**xii, 17, 41-42, 44, 83-84; **4:**87, 88; **5:**24, 27-28; **6:**13, 17, 21
NATO, **6:**67, 69
Near v. Minnesota (1931), **5:**59
Nebraska, **6:**31, 76
Nelson, Samuel, **5:**85

Nelson, Thomas, Jr., **1**:xi, 88-89, 120, 122
New Deal (Franklin Roosevelt program), **5**:57, 63, 95; **6**:65, 67, 73
New Hampshire, **1**:4-5, 6-7, 8-9, 122; **2**:6-7, 8-9, 109, 111; **3**:58-60, 61-63, 131, 132; **4**:4-5, 8, 62, 63, 64-65, 144; **6**:30
New Jersey, **1**:38-39, 40-41, 42-43, 44-45, 46-47, 122, 126; **2**:28-29, 30-31, 32-33, 34-35, 105, 111; **3**:66-68, 69-70, 71-72, 130; **4**:5, 8, 14, 68-69, 70, 71, 72, 134, 144; **6**:46, 57
New Jersey Plan, **2**:30, 32
New Mexico, **6**:29
New Orleans, Battle of (1815), **6**:11, 16, 17
New York, **1**:30-31, 32-33, 34-35, 36-37, 122, 123, 126; **2**:24-25, 104-105, 109, 111; **3**:11, 74-77, 78-80, 131, 133; **4**:5, 6-7, 8, 12, 14, 16, 74-75, 76-77, 78, 79-80, 81, 82, 138; **5**:7, 8, 10, 47-48; **6**:18-19, 28-29, 46-47, 52, 53, 64;
New York City, **3**:15, 133; **4**:7, 11-12, 15; **5**:97
New York Times v. *Sullivan* (1964), **5**:72
Ninth Amendment, **4**:146
Nixon, Richard Milhous, **5**:75, 76, 77, 81; **6**:3, 74-75, 77, 83, 85, 95, 101, 102
Nobel Peace Prize, **6**:53
Non-Importation Agreements, **3**:37
Non-Intercourse Act (1809), **3**:28

Norris, George, **3**:5
North Carolina, **1**:94-95, 96-97, 98-99, 122, 126, 127; **2**:82-83, 84-85, 86-87, 106-107, 111; **3**:28, 82-84, 85-87, 131; **4**:84, 85, 86-87, 88-89, 90, 111-112, 113; **6**:24
Northwest Ordinance (1787), **2**:14
Notes on Virginia (Jefferson), **2**:105
Nuclear Test Ban Treaty, **6**:71
Nullification, **6**:22-23

Oak Hill (James Monroe's home), **3**:117-118
O'Connor, Sandra Day, **5**:78, 88
Ohio, **5**:33; **6**:38, 40, 42, 50, 51, 54, 58
"Old Hickory" (Andrew Jackson's nickname), **6**:16
"Old Man Eloquent" (John Q. Adams' nickname), **6**:15
"Old Rough and Ready" (Zachary Taylor's nickname), **6**:26
Olive Branch Petition, **2**:60-61
Olmstead v. *United States* (1928), **5**:54
Olney, Richard, **6**:47
Open Door policy, **6**:51
Oregon, **6**:41
Osgood, Samuel, **4**:141
Ostend Manifesto (1854), **6**:33
Oswald, Lee Harvey, **6**:71
Otis, James, **1**:94, 95

Paca, William, **1**:74-75, 89, 120, 122

Page, John, **4:**22, 126-127
Paine, Robert Treat, **1:**14-15, 120, 122
Paine, Robert Treat, Jr., **1:**15
Paine, Thomas, **3:**94
Panama Canal, **6:**53, 79
Panic of 1837, **6:**19
Panic of 1893, **6:**47
Parker, Alton B., **6:**100
Parker, Josiah, **4:**128-29
Partridge, George, **4:**57
Patents, **4:**144
Paterson, William, **2:**30, 32-33, 57, 77, 109; **3:**13, 66-68, 69, 126, 129, 130; **5:**3, 22, 84
Paterson's Practice Laws (Paterson), **3:**68
Patronage, **6:**41, 43, 45
Peale, Charles Wilson, **1:**56
Peckham, Rufus W., **5:**86
Pendergast, Thomas, **6:**67
Pendleton, Edmund, **1:**81, 99
"Penman of the Revolution" (John Dickinson's nickname), **2:**60
Penn, John, **1:**98-99, 120, 122; **3:**93
Penn, Thomas, **3:**90
Pennsylvania, **1:**48-49, 50-51, 52-53, 54-55, 56-57, 58-59, 60-61, 62-63, 64-65, 122, 126; **2:**38-39, 40-41, 42-43, 44-45, 46-47, 48-49, 50-51, 52-53, 111; **3:**90-92, 93-95, 130; **4:**5, 8, 92-93, 94, 95, 96, 97-98, 99, 101, 102, 144; **6:**32
People's Party, **6:**100
Perkins, Frances, **6:**64
Perry, Matthew C., **6:**29
Philadelphia, **2:**46; **3:**15, 72, 133; **4:**138, 139; **5:**97

Philadelphia Convention. *See* Constitutional Convention (1787)
Philippines, **5:**52; **6:**51
Pickering, Timothy, **3:**62
Pierce, Franklin, **6:**2, 30-31, 33, 99
Pierce, William, **2:**14, 20, 28, 34, 57, 58, 62, 65, 77, 83, 94, 100, 107; **3:**32, 67, 106
Pinchot, Gifford, **6:**55
Pinckney, Charles (1757-1824), **2:**92, 94-95, 108
Pinckney, Charles Cotesworth (1746-1825), **1:**17; **2:**14, 62, 92-93, 108; **6:**98
Pinckney, Elizabeth, **2:**92
Pinckney, Thomas, **2:**92
Pitney, Mahlon, **5:**86
Plain Dealer, The, **3:**72
Plessy v. *Ferguson* (1896), **5:**44
Political parties, **6:**7, 89, 90
  presidential candidates, **6:**97-102
  See also specific parties
Polk, James Knox, **6:**24-25, 27, 31, 33, 99
Pollock v. *Farmers' Loan & Trust Co.* (1895), **5:**44
Poor Richard's Almanac (Franklin), **2:**39
Populist Party. *See* People's Party
Pornography, **5:**82
Powell, Lewis F., Jr., **5:**88
Presidency
  biographies, **6:**4-85
  death in office, **6:**20, 27, 35, 43, 51, 59, 65, 71, 95-96
  elections (*see* Presidential elections)
  first inaugural, **4:**15-16

inaugural date, **6:**94-95
nonconsecutive terms, **6:**46
origins and development,
  6:1-3
pensions, **6:**67
powers given, **3:**8-9; **6:**2
prior to George Washington,
  6:86-87
resignation, **6:**75, 95
succession issue, **6:**23
term length, **6:**94-96
third party candidacy, **6:**53
Presidential elections
  candidates, **6:**97-102
  Electoral College and, **6:**7, 9,
    15, 16, 41, 49, 88-93
Proclamation of Neutrality
  (1793), **3:**17; **4:**85
Profiles in Courage (Kennedy),
  6:71
Progressive Party, **6:**53, 101
Prohibition Party, **6:**99, 100
Property rights, **5:**27, 29, 37,
  39, 39-40, 42
Puerto Rico, **6:**51
Pullman Strike (1894), **5:**44;
  6:47
Pure Food and Drug Act, **5:**49

Quakers, **2:**40, 41; **3:**105, 108;
  4:36, 38, 126, 136

Radical Republicans, **5:**33, 34;
  6:37
Railroads, **6:**41, 45, 47
Randolph, Anne Carey, **2:**53
Randolph, Edmund, **2:**94, 105-
  106, 109; **4:**5, 116, 140; **5:**2,
  22
Randolph, Peyton, **6:**86

Randolph, Thomas Mann, **2:**53
Read, George, **1:**viii, 67, 68-69,
  120, 122; **2:**56-57; **3:**13, 36-
  38, 123, 124, 126, 130
Reagan, Ronald Wilson, **5:**80;
  6:77, 80-81, 91, 102
Reconstruction, **5:**34, 94; **6:**37,
  41
Reconstruction Finance Cor-
  poration, **6:**63
*Records of the Federal Conven-
  tion* (Farrand), **5:**89
Reed, Stanley F., **5:**87
Reed, Thomas B., **6:**49
Regulator War (1765-1771),
  2:100; **3:**41, 86
Rehnquist, William Hubbs,
  5:23, 29, 79-83, 88
Republican Party (founded
  1854), **5:**33; **6:**33, 35, 41,
  43, 44-45, 49, 53, 55, 57, 61,
  69, 75, 77, 81, 83, 91, 99,
  100, 101, 102
Republican Party (Jefferson-
  ian). *See* Democratic-
  Republican Party
Revolutionary War, **1:**7, 89; **2:**2,
  6, 24, 40, 42, 45, 46, 90, 92,
  94; **3:**19, 70, 79, 93, 112-
  113, 115, 116-117, 123, 126;
  4:32, 111, 128; **6:**6
Reynold v. *Sims* (1964), **5:**72
Rhode Island, **1:**18-19, 20-21,
  122; **2:**109, 111; **3:**28, 98-
  100, 101-102, 120, 131;
  4:104, 144
Rickover, Hyman, **6:**78
Roberts, Owen J., **5:**87
Robinson, John, **1:**83, 93
Rockefeller, Nelson, **6:**77
Rodney, Caesar, **1:**xi, 66-67, 68,
  70, 120

Roe v. *Wade* (1973), **5:**76, 81
Rogers, John, **1:**122, 124
Roosevelt, Eleanor, **6:**64
Roosevelt, Franklin Delano, **5:**60, 62, 63, 95-96; **6:**2, 64-65, 70, 95, 101
Roosevelt, Theodore, **5:**44, 53; **6:**2, 49, 52-53, 55, 65, 96, 100
Rosecrans, William, **6:**43
Rosenberg, Julius and Ethel, **5:**68
Ross, George, **1:**64-65, 69, 120, 125; **2:**56
Rough Riders, **6:**53
Rush, Benjamin, **1:**9, 40, 50-51, 120, 125; **2:**68
Russo-Japanese War, **6:**53
Rutledge, Edward, **1:**ix, xi, 100-101, 103, 120, 122; **2:**90
Rutledge, John, **1:**ix, 124; **2:**62, 90-91, 109; **4:**108; **5:**11-14, 84
Rutledge, Wiley H., **5:**87

St. Clair, Arthur, **6:**87
St. John, John P., **6:**99
Sanford, Edward T., **5:**87
San Juan Hill, Battle of (1898), **6:**53
Santa Anna (Mexican general), **6:**27
Santa Clara County v. *Southern Pacific Railroad Co.* (1886), **5:**39-40
Scalia, Antonin, **5:**81, 88
Schechter Poultry Corp. v. *United States* (1935), **5:**59
Schureman, James, **4:**71
Schuyler, Philip, **1:**123; **2:**24; **3:**78-80, 126, 131

Scott, Thomas, **4:**12, 100
Scott, Winfield, **6:**38, 99
SEATO, **6:**69
Secession, **5:**34
Second Amendment, **4:**54-55
Sedgwick, Theodore, **4:**21, 58-59, 133, 137
Seminole Wars, **6:**26
Senate
  Bill of Rights, **3:**127
  closed sessions, **4:**13
  compensation, **3:**133
  creation of, **3:**1-6; **6:**7
  first (*see* First Senate)
  outstanding senators **3:**xi
  powers granted to, **3:**7-9
  punishment degrees, **3:**5
  qualifications, **3:**3-4
Seney, Joshua, **4:**46
Separate but equal doctrine, **5:**43, 68, 71
Separation of powers, **3:**90; **5:**1, 2
Seventeenth Amendment, **2:**84
Sevier, John, **4:**86-87
Seward, William H., **6:**27
Seymour, Horatio, **6:**99
Shay's Rebellion (1786), **2:**ix, 3; **4:**50
Sherman, John, **6:**43
Sherman, Roger, **1:**viii, 22-23, 112, 120, 122, 125; **2:**20-21, 28, 30; **3:**127; **4:**5, 20, 21, 23, 27-28
Sherman, William, **6:**49
Sherman Anti-Trust Act (1890), **5:**44, 49
Shippen, William, **1:**50
Shiras, George, **5:**86
"Silent Cal" (Coolidge nickname), **6:**61
Silver issue, **6:**41, 47, 51

Silvester, Peter, **4**:81
Sinnickson, Thomas, **4**:72
Sixteenth Amendment, **5**:44
Sketch of the Creek Country (Hawkins), **3**:84
Slaughterhouse Cases (1873), **5**:35, 39
Slavery, **1**:7, 81; **2**:28, 97, 100, 108; **3**:27, 102; **4**:36, 107, 109-110, 113, 126, 136; **5**:29-30; **6**:27, 31, 37
  opponents, **1**:19, 21, 83; **2**:14, 101; **3**:75, 77; **4**:58, 60; **5**:32-33; **6**:29, 35
  supporters, **2**:103; **3**:105, 108, 124, 126; **4**:38; **5**:13, 24; **6**:27, 33
Smith, Alfred E., **6**:65, 101
Smith, James, **1**:58-59, 120, 125
Smith, Melancton, **2**:24-25
Smith, William (Maryland congressman), **4**:47
Smith, William Loughton (South Carolina congressman), **4**:109-110, 136
Socialist Party, **6**:100, 101
Society of Friends. *See* Quakers
Souter, David, **5**:88
South Carolina, **1**:100-101, 102-103, 104-105, 106-107, 122, 123; **2**:90-91, 92-93, 94-95, 96-97, 111; **3**:104-106, 107-109, 131; **4**:5, 8, 106-107, 108, 109-110, 144; **5**:12; **6**:41, 90
Spaight, Richard Dobbs, **2**:84-85
Spain, **2**:95; **3**:xii; **6**:51, 53
Spanish-American War, **6**:51, 53
Speaker of the House, first, **4**:12-13

Square Deal (Theodore Roosevelt program), **6**:53
"Stalwarts" (Republican Party faction), **6**:43, 45
Stamp Act (1765), **1**:3, 9, 25, 33, 44-45, 83; **2**:60; **3**:30, 37, 47, 86, 93
Stanly, John, **2**:84-85
Stanton, Joseph, **3**:99, 101-102, 123, 126, 131
Stare decisis, **5**:76, 81
"Star Spangled Banner, The" (national anthem), **2**:69; **6**:11
State of Franklin, **4**:86
State sovereignty theory, **5**:23-24
States' rights, **3**:2-3; **6**:23
States' Rights Party, **6**:101
Steele, John, **4**:88-89
Stevens, John Paul, **5**:88
Stevens Gas Commission, **5**:57-58
Stevenson, Adlai E., **6**:91
Stewart, Potter, **5**:88
Stockton, Richard, **1**:xi, 12, 38-39, 51, 120, 122; **2**:32; **3**:66
Stone, Harlan Fiske, **5**:19, 59, 61-64, 87, 99
Stone, Michael Jenifer, **4**:48
Stone, Thomas, **1**:ix, 76-77, 120, 122
Story, Joseph, **4**:21; **5**:24, 25, 28, 84
Streeter, Anson J., **6**:100
Stromberg v. California (1931), **5**:59
Strong, Caleb, **2**:104; **3**:13, 54-56, 126, 130
Strong, William, **5**:85
Sturges, Jonathan, **4**:29
Suffolk Resolves, **1**:126

Index / 159

Sullivan, John, **1:**37; **2:**34
Sumter, Thomas, **4:**111-112
Supreme Court
   Chief Justices (*see* Chief Justices)
   circuit duties, **5:**9, 43, 90, 93-94
   convening practice, **5:**49
   creation of, **5:**1-4
   first meeting, **5:**8
   first session, **5:**97
   judicial review power, **5:**89-92
   justices, **5:**84-88
   meeting places, **5:**97-99
   multiple concurring opinions, **5:**64
   packing plan, **5:**60
   size, **5:**93-96
Sutherland, George, **5:**87
Swallow, Silas C., **6:**100
Swayne, Noah H., **5:**85
Sweatt v. Painter (1950), **5:**68
Sweeney, George W., **1:**81

Taft, Alonzo, **6:**54
Taft, Robert A. 3.xi
Taft, William Howard, **5:**48, 49, 51-55, 58, 87, 99; **6:**53, 54-55, 100
Taney, Roger Brooke, **5:**26-30, 85
Tariffs, **2:**46, 108; **3:**41, 47, 59; **6:**25, 43, 47, 49, 51, 55, 57
Taylor, George, **1:**60-61, 120, 125
Taylor, Zachary, **6:**25, 26-27, 29, 38, 95, 99
Tecumseh (Shawnee chief), **6:**21
Tennessee, **4:**86; **6:**17, 24, 36-37

Tenth Amendment, **4:**146
Texas, **6:**23, 25, 29, 72
Thacher, George, **4:**60
Thanksgiving, **4:**131
Third Amendment, **4:**23
Thomas, Clarence, **5:**88
Thomas, Norman, **6:**101
Thompson, Smith, **5:**84
Thornton, Matthew, **1:**8-9, 120, 124, 125
Thurmond, J. Strom, **6:**101
Tilden, Samuel J., **6:**41, 99
Tilghman, Matthew, **1:**124
"Tippecanoe and Tyler Too," **6:**21
Todd, Thomas, **5:**84
"Trail of Tears," **6:**17
Trimble, Robert, **5:**84
Truman, Harry S, **5:**66, 68; **6:**2, 63, 66-67, 69, 95, 96, 101
Truman Doctrine, **6:**67
Trumbull, John, **1:**26
Trumbull, Jonathan, **1:**26, 28; **2:**18; **4:**30-31, 98, 140, 142
Tryon, William, **2:**100
Tucker, Thomas Tudor, **4:**22, 113, 131
Tuckerman, Bayard, **3:**80
Turner, James, **2:**85
Turner v. Bank of North America, **5:**18
Twelfth Amendment, **2:**96; **6:**89
Twentieth Amendment, **3:**5; **6:**94
Twenty-seventh Amendment, **4:**144
Twenty-third Amendment, **6:**92
Tyler, John, **6:**22-23, 96

Union Labor Party, **6:**100
Union Party (1864), **6:**37, 99

Union Party (1936), **6:**101
United Nations, **6:**65, 83
United States of America in Congress Assembled, **6:**86, 87
United States v. E. C. Knight Co. (1895), **5:**44
United States v. Lopez (1995), **5:**83
United States v. Nixon (1974), **5:**76-77
United States v. Peters (1809), **5:**23-24
University of Pennsylvania, **3:**69-70
Utah, **6:**29

Van Buren, Martin, **6:**18-19, 21, 98, 99
Van Devanter, Willis, **5:**53, 86
Van Rensselaer, Jeremiah, **4:**82
Van Rensselaer, Stephen, **2:**33
Vermont, **4:**141, 145; **6:**44, 60
Vice President
 election of, **6:**89, 91
 presidential succession, **6:**95-96
Vietnam War, **6:**73, 75, 85
Vining, John, **4:**21, 23, 36, 140
Vinson, Frederick Moore, **5:**65-68, 72, 87
Virginia, **1:**80-81, 82-83, 84-85, 86-87, 88-89, 90-91, 92-93, 122, 126, 127; **2:**2-3, 76-77, 78-79, 105-106, 111; **3:**11, 112-113, 114-115, 116-118, 119-121, 131, 133; **4:**5, 5-6, 7, 8-10, 116, 117, 118, 119, 120, 121-122, 123-124, 125, 126-127, 128-129, 130, 135, 138, 143-144, 145; **6:**5, 8, 10, 12, 20, 22, 26, 56
Virginia Plan, **2:**32; **5:**2; **6:**1, 88
Virginia Resolutions, **1:**127

Wadsworth, Jerimiah, **4:**32-33
Waite, Morrison Remick, **5:**34, 36-41, 85
Walker, John, **3:**114-115, 124, 126, 131
Wallace, George C., **6:**101
Wallace, Henry A., **6:**101
Walton, George, **1:**xi, 112-113, 121, 122
Ware v. Hylton (1796), **5:**18, 22
War of 1812, **2:**68-69; **3:**15, 62, 76, 84; **5:**98; **6:**11, 21
Warren, Earl, **5:**69-73, 88
Warren Commission, **5:**73
Washington, Bushrod, **5:**84
Washington, D.C.
 planning, **2:**73; **3:**14; **4:**43-44, 121, 138; **5:**98
 Senate home, **3:**15-16, 134
 Supreme Court home, **5:**97, 98-99
 voting rights, **6:**92
Washington, George, **2:**43; **3:**53, 75, 114; **4:**5, 11; **5:**7, 22; **6:**89
 at Constitutional Convention, **2:**2-3, 42; **4:**3; **6:**4-5
 presidency, **2:**52, 68, 77; **3:**20, 59, 68, 76, 91, 117; **4:**6, 14, 15-16, 22, 88, 132-133, 138, 140, 141; **5:**8-9, 13, 16, 93; **6:**9, 13, 94, 95, 97
 Revolutionary War, **1:**39; **2:**24, 40; **3:**1, 79, 112-113, 115, 132; **6:**6

Index / 161

Washington Naval Treaty, **6:**59
Watergate, **6:**75
Wayne, Anthony, **4:**39
Wayne, James M., **5:**85
Weaver, James B., **6:**99, 100
Webster, Daniel, **3:**xi, 74; **6:**21, 98
Weed, Thurlow, **6:**28-29
Wheaton, Joseph, **4:**17
Whig Party, **6:**21, 23, 25, 27, 28-29, 33, 35, 97, 98, 99
Whipple, William, **1:**6-7, 121, 122
Whiskey Rebellion (1794), **2:**33, 40; **3:**20; **4:**139; **6:**5
White, Alexander, **4:**121, 130, 138, 139
White, Byron R., **5:**88
White, Edward Douglass, **5:**46-50, 62, 86
White, Hugh L., **6:**98
Whitefield, George, **3:**34
White House, **5:**98; **6:**11
Whittaker, Charles E., **5:**88
Why England Slept (Kennedy), **6:**71
Williams, William, **1:**26-27, 121, 125
Williamson, Hugh, **2:**62, 86-87, 108; **4:**90
Willing, Thomas, **1:**122, 123; **3:**93, 94
Willkie, Wendell, **6:**101
Wilson, James, **1:**viii, 62-63, 121, 122; **2:**12, 38, 50-51, 77, 109; **5:**17, 84; **6:**88
Wilson, Woodrow, **5:**58; **6:**2, 56-57, 65, 100
Wingate, Paine, **3:**13, 61-63, 124, 126, 131
Wirt, William, **6:**98
Wiscart v. *Dauchy* (1796), **5:**18
Wisner, Henry, **1:**122, 123
Witherspoon, John, **1:**39, 40-41, 121, 122
Wolcott, Oliver, **1:**28-29, 121, 124
Wolcott, Oliver, Jr., **1:**29
Woodbury, Levi, **5:**85
Woods, William B., **5:**85
Wooley, John C., **6:**100
Worcester v. *Georgia* (1832), **5:**24
World War I, **6:**57, 67
World War II, **6:**65, 67, 68-69, 71, 75, 76, 81, 82, 95
Wright, James, **1:**110
Wynkoop, Henry, **4:**98, 101
Wythe, George, **1:**viii, 80-81, 121, 124; **2:**106, 108; **5:**21

XYZ Affair, **2:**93; **4:**53, 119; **5:**22

Yates, Robert, **2:**24, 104-105, 109
Yazoo Land Act, **4:**40